Debating Rights Inflation in Canada

Canadian Commentaries

Published in conjunction with the *Literary Review of Canada*, Canadian Commentaries features prominent writers exploring key issues affecting Canadians and the world. A lead essay commissioned by the *LRC* becomes the ground for responses by others, opening a place for a spectrum of views and debate.

We welcome manuscripts from Canadian authors. For further information, please contact the Series Editor:

Dr. Janice Gross Stein
Director, Munk Centre for International Studies
University of Toronto
1 Devonshire Place
Toronto, ON M5S 3K7
Canada
Phone: (416) 946-8908
Fax: (416) 946-8915
Email: j.stein@utoronto.ca

Debating Rights Inflation in Canada
A Sociology of Human Rights

Dominique Clément

With contributions from
Nathalie Des Rosiers
Pearl Eliadis
Rhoda E. Howard-Hassmann
Gert Verschraegen

WILFRID LAURIER
UNIVERSITY PRESS

Inspiring Lives.

Wilfrid Laurier University Press acknowledges the support of the Canada Council for the Arts for our publishing program. We acknowledge the financial support of the Government of Canada through the Canada Book Fund for our publishing activities. This work was supported by the Research Support Fund.

Canada Council for the Arts   Conseil des arts du Canada

ONTARIO ARTS COUNCIL
CONSEIL DES ARTS DE L'ONTARIO
an Ontario government agency
un organisme du gouvernement de l'Ontario

Library and Archives Canada Cataloguing in Publication

Clément, Dominique, [date], author
    Debating rights inflation in Canada : a sociology of human rights / Dominique Clément ; with contributions from Nathalie Des Rosiers, Pearl Eliadis, Rhoda E. Howard-Hassmann, Gert Verschraegen.

(Canadian commentaries)
Includes bibliographical references and index. Issued in print and electronic formats.

ISBN 978-1-77112-244-3 (softcover).—ISBN 978-1-77112-276-4 (EPUB).—ISBN 978-1-77112-275-7 (PDF)

    1. Human rights—Social aspects—Canada. I. Title. II. Series: Canadian commentaries

JC599.C3C54152016   323.0971   C2018-903152-2
                                             C2018-903153-0

Cover design by Daiva Villa, Chris Rowat Design. Interior design by Angela Booth Malleau.

This book is printed on FSC® certified paper and is certified Ecologo. It contains post-consumer fibre, is processed chlorine free, and is manufactured using biogas energy. This book is printed on FSC® certified paper and is certified Ecologo. It contains post-consumer fibre, is processed chlorine free, and is manufactured using biogas energy.

Printed in Canada

RECYCLED
Paper made from recycled material
FSC   FSC® C103567
www.fsc.org

Contents

Additional Resources   vii
Preface   ix
Introduction   1

Rights Inflation in Canada   19

Commentary
The Right Investment in Rights   79
Nathalie Des Rosiers

Commentary
Too Many Rights?   97
Pearl Eliadis

Commentary
Liberalism, Social Democracy, and Human Rights   121
Rhoda E. Howard-Hassmann

Commentary
Historical Contingency and Human Rights Pluralism   133
Gert Verschraegen

Contributors   145
Index   149

Additional Resources

Canada's Human Rights History
www.HistoryOfRights.ca

Canada's Human Rights History is a site dedicated to exploring every aspect of Canada's rights revolution. It is a research and teaching portal for the study of social movements, state policy, and law. In addition to providing information on critical human rights moments and controversies throughout Canadian history, the site provides access to an extensive collection of archival materials. The site also contains detailed reading lists, links to other resources, and information on conferences, publications, research funding, and recent events. Unlike most historical websites, this site is not static but, rather, new content is added as the author's scholarship evolves.

Preface

The essay and commentator responses in this book were written for a broad audience. This book was inspired, in part, by the author's participation on the Canadian Museum for Human Rights' National Advisory Council. It also builds on a report commissioned by the Canadian Human Rights Commission on the evolution of human rights in Canada. It will be of interest to people in Canada and abroad, as well as to non-specialists who are new to the field of human rights. It brings together activists, scholars, and human rights practitioners. Our hope is that this debate benefits not only scholars of human rights but also those people who engage every day in putting human rights into practice.

Our objective was to foster a debate between the author and the commentators. The essay that forms the premise of this book is provocative. Commentators were encouraged to be critical in their responses. Because we wanted to focus this book on the idea of rights inflation and its implications, we had to make some difficult choices. Readers will note that the main essay provides only a cursory examination of the history of human rights in Canada. Yet a significant aspect of the argument rests on the premise that certain core rights have always informed Canadian rights talk. It would have been impossible, though, to discuss in greater detail the history of Canada's rights culture. Certainly, doing so would have required focusing less on the implications of rights inflation, which is the purpose of this book. In this regard, a useful complement to this book is the author's website www.HistoryOfRights.ca or his book *Human Rights in Canada: A History*. The discussion on core rights and history is, in part, drawn from that book.

Introduction

Human rights practitioners face hard choices every day. In 2005, as a member of the British Columbia Civil Liberties Association's board of directors, I found myself in the midst of a debate over whether or not to intervene in a controversial child pornography case. A teenage boy who had taken naked pictures of his girlfriend on his cellphone had, following an acrimonious breakup, decided to enact retribution by distributing the images on the Internet. Because the girl was underage, the Crown decided to charge the young man, who was also underage, with distribution of child pornography. A comparable but far more horrific case made headlines eight years later in Halifax. Two teenage boys were charged with distributing child pornography following the suicide of Rehtaeh Parsons. One of the boys had taken a photo of the other sexually assaulting Parsons at a party. She was fifteen years old. Parsons later killed herself after a photo of the assault was circulated on social media. Both boys pleaded guilty. Nova Scotia later passed (unanimously) the *Cyber-Safety Act* in 2014 to prohibit online bullying.[1]

Charging teens with creating and distributing child pornography is a creative use of the law. It is also a disturbing interpretation of a provision in the *Criminal Code* that was never intended to target youthful offenders. The original case had generated an emotional debate among the directors. Some people thought that the heinous nature of the act, and the failure of the law to protect innocent victims, justified such an unorthodox use of the law. Others believed that the failure lay with lawmakers and that we should oppose the charge in order to demonstrate the need for legal reform. The most noteworthy moment in the debate, however, arose when someone asked whether the charge violated the boy's human rights under the *Canadian Charter of Rights and Freedoms*. Only a few of the directors at the meeting were lawyers. Yet it was fascinating to see how that one question immediately silenced what had been, until that moment, a lively exchange. For the next thirty minutes the rest of us became mere spectators as the lawyers discussed precedent, legislative interpretation, and the courts. What had begun for me as a profoundly moral issue had somehow turned into an exclusively legal debate. It seemed as if the issue of whether or not the young man's legal rights were being violated had taken paramount importance. It was a powerful lesson on the nature of the law and rights discourse.

The association of human rights with the law, and the tendency to disagree over the meaning of rights, are among the central themes in this book. The main essay asks two questions in particular: How have Canadians understood human rights in the past compared to today? And what are the consequences of rights inflation, which is the tendency to frame almost any grievance as a human rights violation? The central premise of the essay is that since the 1970s, human rights have become the common vernacular for framing anything that is deemed an injustice. What are the implications, therefore, of failing to distinguish between human rights, which should be the highest possible claim upon our society, and any grievance that we feel is an injustice?

Legal scholars and political philosophers have long dominated the study of human rights. I take an historical and sociological approach. For most of Canadian history, people were more likely to talk about rights in reference to, for example, British justice rather than human rights. Such a narrow conception of rights, which was associated with citizenship rather than humanity, limited those grievances that people were prone to frame as rights violations. References to political freedoms (speech, association, assembly, press), the right to vote, religious freedom, equal treatment, and due process dominated rights talk in Canada until recent history.[2] I argue that these core rights have always been integral to our rights vernacular.[3] This is not to suggest that core rights have priority over other claims. It is not an argument for creating hierarchies of rights. Nor am I suggesting that my list of core rights is exhaustive. I am not seeking to defend a list of rights in order to exclude other rights claims. Rather, I identify rights that have always been integral to rights talk in Canada for the purpose of demonstrating the profound impact that the popularization of human rights in the 1970s has had on rights talk in Canada.

As the recent scholarship on the history of human rights has demonstrated, the instinct to frame almost any grievance as a rights violation is a historically unique development.[4] The term "human rights" was not integral to Canadians' rights vernacular for a great part of our history. Most law schools in Canada and the United States did not even offer courses on human rights until the 1980s or later.[5] Similarly, a search of the term "human rights" in the *Globe and Mail* newspaper shows a graph that remains flat for most of 1859 to 1940, a slight rise between 1940 and 1960, and then a dramatic jump in the 1970s. It is the same with other major newspapers, such as the *Toronto Star* and the *Winnipeg Free Press*: a remarkable escalation in the 1970s of the print media using the term human rights to frame grievances. The popularization of this vernacular since the 1970s has encouraged people to frame a much broader range of grievances as rights violations. To be sure, Canadians have been advocating around issues such as poverty, health care, and the environment for generations. It is far more common, however, to hear such grievances framed today as human rights violations than it was in the past. As a result, rights inflation, the tendency to frame almost any grievance as a rights violation, has transformed rights talk in Canada.

Human rights are most apparent in those rights that are codified in law. But rights are more than the law. To have social meaning, they must be embedded in institutions and social practice. A sociology of human rights is concerned with identifying how rights are practised in society. For this reason, many sociologists define rights as claims made by people against established power arrangements to protect their dignity.[6] This might include people submitting complaints to human rights commissions or arguing a case in court. Or people posting messages on social media or writing about human rights on blogs or in newspapers. It might also include social movement organizations that frame their grievances as human rights violations. Or how people talk about human rights in schools and museums.

The advent of what Louis Henkin called the "age of rights," however, has resulted in what several scholars refer to as "rights inflation" or the proliferation of rights.[7] Rights inflation is the process through which new rights claims emerge.[8] It takes the form of either redefining recognized rights or seeking recognition of entirely new rights. Our rights culture is, in this way, constantly evolving. Rights inflation manifests itself in myriad ways: governments that pass legislation; judges who overturn legislation or make new law; state administrative tribunals that offer new interpretations of policy or law; changes in public discourse around rights; or social movements and individuals who frame their grievances as rights in a way that captures the popular imagination.[9] Human rights have also evolved beyond claims against the state. We assert rights against attempts by social systems to reduce our individual autonomy, whether it involves criticizing how businesses regulate employees or asserting our gender identity in school.

Rights inflation need not be problematic. In fact, it is essential that human rights adapt to new contexts. Still, there is a danger in framing any and all grievances as rights violations. In 1983 the renowned philosopher H.L.A. Hart suggested that the "doctrine of human rights has at least temporarily replaced the doctrine of maximizing utilitarianism as the prime philosophical inspiration of political and social reform."[10] More recently, Mirko Bagaric and James Allan have observed that there is now "a strong tendency to advance virtually all moral claims and arguments in terms of rights."[11] Similarly, Florian Hoffman argues that "human rights has come to enjoy a near monopoly on emancipatory and utopian

This is not an old debate. More recently, philosopher James Griffin has lamented that the widespread use of rights talk has made it a "debased" rhetoric.[19] Political scientist Amy Gutmann has insisted that the "proliferation of human rights to include rights that are not clearly necessary to protect the basic agency or needs or dignity of persons cheapens the purpose of human rights."[20] Eric Posner, in a book on international law, describes the "hypertrophy of rights" as the proliferation of rights in a way that renders them meaningless for constraining states' behaviour: "[rights proliferation] does not represent a triumph of human rights ... The more human rights there are, and thus the greater the variety of human interests that are protected, the more that the human rights system collapses into an undifferentiated welfarism in which all interests must be taken seriously for the sake of the public good."[21] Connor Gearty, the former director of the Centre for the Study of Human Rights at the London School of Economics, argues that "the human rights tent should not be so broad that everybody can be squeezed into it, and some interest groups and advocates will be surprised, angry indeed, to be left outside."[22] Sociologists Gideon Sjoberg, Elizabeth A. Gill, and Norma Williams similarly argue that "there is a grave danger that if we speak glibly about human rights, we may lose sight of the reality that some rights are more basic than others."[23] Legal scholars and activists Rose Freedman and Jacob Mchangama suggest that the proliferation of Special Procedure mandates at the United Nations is designed to undermine investigations into widespread rights abuses by spreading out limited resources.[24] Aryeh Neier, a co-founder of Human Rights Watch and later president of Open Society, has long been a vocal opponent of an expansive definition of human rights.[25]

Scholars who critique rights inflation or the proliferation of human rights base their arguments on the premise that there are basic or core rights.[26] Michael Ignatieff, a prominent public intellectual on rights, warns that "rights inflation—the tendency to define anything desirable as a right—ends up eroding the legitimacy of a defensible core of rights."[27] He defines core rights as those basic civil and political liberties that are necessary to protecting human agency.[28] Neier embraces a similar definition of human rights.[29] Amartya Sen, a Nobel Prize–winning economist, argues that certain rights, such as free speech, are a precondition for other rights. Famines do not occur, Sen argues, in societies with open government and a free press.[30] Philip Alston identified a series of core rights that were almost universally recognized in constitutions that incorporated human rights provisions such as "the right to life, freedom from torture, freedom from arbitrary arrest and detention, the right to be presumed innocent, the right to privacy, freedom of movement, the right to property, freedom of thought, conscience, and religion, freedom of expression, freedom of assembly and association, and the right to participate in government."[31] Brian Grodsky defines core rights in association with integrity of the person, specifically "violations including arbitrary arrest, disappearance, detention, torture and political killing."[32] And James Griffith argues that human rights should be only the minimum necessary to ensure human agency: autonomy, welfare (e.g., security of the person), liberty (e.g., expression), privacy, and asylum.[33]

Debates surrounding rights inflation, as well as the notion of core or basic rights, have been a mainstay of political philosophy and legal studies for many years. In this book, by contrast, we engage in this debate from a historical and sociological perspective. A sociological approach does not approach rights as an abstract principle that exists outside society; rather, it is premised on the belief that "individual rights are constructed by and in society; the individual and the social are mutually constitutive of one another, rather than the individual being ontologically prior to the social, as is implicitly assumed in the natural rights tradition."[34] I consider how rights manifest themselves in social practice using Canada as a case study. My discussion of core rights is, to be sure, not exhaustive. Political philosophers such as Gutmann or Shue, for instance, embrace the notion of core rights but would include the right to subsistence where others do not. Unlike Gutmann or Shue, however, I am not attempting to formulate a foundational moral philosophy of rights. I do not include subsistence on my list of core rights simply because there is no evidence that subsistence was integral to rights talk in Canada in the past. Discussing those core rights that have always informed rights talk in Canada is a way of beginning a conversation around what grievances are today best framed as human rights violations (rather than as social justice).[35]

In the first section of the main essay I discuss the history of rights talk in Canada. As sociologists Mikael Madsen and Gert Verschraegen explain, although there are historical precedents in religious or cultural traditions for many of the principles underlying rights, a society organized around human rights principles is a modern invention: "There is nothing natural, let alone inevitable, about ordering societies around the idea of universally equal and inalienable human rights."[36] I place particular emphasis on how rights talk has changed in recent history. Although historians are still relatively new to this field of study, a common theme in this emerging scholarship is that the idea of human rights did not gain widespread popularity until the 1970s.[37]

Human rights are historically contingent. In part, this means that certain societal preconditions facilitated the popularization of human rights. The idea of human rights emerged as a response to new threats and possibilities associated with the advent of democracy and capitalism. A modern industrial economy combined with a powerful state produces social disruptions arising from mass education, geographic mobility, and segmented family units. Such disruptions to social networks and the emphasis on individual autonomy facilitated the popularization of human rights as a way of framing grievances. The proliferation of rights talk coincided with the growing repressive capacity of the state and the emergence of expansive state bureaucracies. The sense of alienation that accompanies the lack of direct control over state institutions makes individual rights a compelling frame.[38]

In this way, rights are not independent of history. They are a distinct social practice that emerged at a particular moment in time. The recognition of workers' rights emerged in the wake of industrialization, and recognition of women's rights in employment emerged after women entered the workforce in large numbers. The claim of a right to education was made possible by the elimination of child labour and the creation of free and compulsory education in the twentieth century.[39] Moreover, human rights are historically contingent because how we interpret and apply these principles changes over time. As historian Lynn Hunt explains, rights talk contains an implacable inner logic.[40] If people successfully appropriate rights discourse in seeking redress for their grievances, it inspires others to do the same.[41] When Catholics and Protestants secured rights around practising their religion in Canada, it was inevitable that religious minorities would demand the same rights. In this way, human rights inevitably evolve over time. There were clear distinctions between rights in the nineteenth century—women were given property rights long before the right to vote. The principle of free speech did not include, at one point in our history, the right to criticize the state. Today, however, we see such rights as interconnected.[42]

As the brief examination of the history of rights talk at the beginning of the main essay demonstrates, it is apparent that certain core rights have always been integral to our rights culture. For this reason, in the following section I show how the meaning and application of core rights remain the source of intense debate and division within society. More importantly, that section shows that rights inflation can be an essential and healthy part of public life. I discuss a handful of recent debates over core rights to show how people challenge society's interpretation and application of these principles. Claims of discrimination and demands for equal treatment, in particular, challenge us by suggesting new ways of thinking about rights.

Rights inflation becomes problematic, however, when it becomes common to frame any and all grievances as rights violations. In the next section, I discuss the widespread use of rights talk today. Compared to the recent past, a remarkable range of grievances are now framed as rights violations. This becomes apparent if we understand rights as they are practised in society and not simply as an abstract principle. A sociology of human rights is premised on the idea that rights "should be firmly linked to the capacity of the state and society at large to guarantee the enjoyment of those rights."[43] To have social meaning, rights must be embedded in social life, from families to courts, governments, schools, and other institutions. I offer examples of how people have used print and social media, human rights commissions, public hearings around the Canadian Museum for Human Rights, the courts, and social movement organizations to reframe long-standing grievances as human rights violations. There is a common bias in legal studies that focuses on the institutionalization of human rights, especially within government and the courts. Yet as Madsen and Verschraegen note, legal measures "can only be effective if they are supported by an underlying institutional infrastructure and cultural values."[44] Newspapers, social media, and advocacy are just three of the venues wherein that we can try to understand how rights are understood and practised in society. As we will see, many emerging rights claims have no historical precedent. Claims for recognizing (and codifying in law) a human right to information, to social services, or to a healthy environment never had the type of popular appeal in the past as they do today.

Finally, I consider the implications of framing systemic social problems as human rights violations. Human rights, I suggest, is a poor way of framing many of these grievances. I argue that we should consider issues such as poverty or environmental degradation as violations of social justice rather than human rights. This by no means suggests that poverty is any less significant than, say, free speech. Rather, it is a debate over how best to frame systemic social problems in ways that produce a vision for social change. Social justice relates to those conditions that enable individuals to pursue their vision of the good life. Illiteracy, poverty, lack of education or health care, and unemployment are violations of social justice because they restrict individuals' capacity to pursue their desires. It has become common to frame issues of social justice as human rights.[45] But social justice and human rights are not the same. If social justice is a dialogue around grievances against the state and society, then human rights are those principles that make the dialogue possible.[46]

Charles Beitz has similarly argued that human rights should not be equated with social justice. He suggests that human rights are a subset of social justice that have priority over other claims rooted in economic, social, political, and cultural context:

> One might be tempted to hold that human rights simply *are* the rights of social justice. This, however, cannot be right ... Human rights are matters of international concern and it is not plausible that the international community should take responsibility for the justice of its component societies. For one thing, requirements of justice are grounded in the interests of different degrees of urgency and therefore exert claims of different weights ... Secondly, some requirements of justice may not be achievable by means of any permissible form of action ... Finally, it is not unreasonable to expect the requirements of social justice, at the level of institutions, laws, and policies, to vary across societies in ways that respond to differences in the economic, social, and cultural background.[47]

My own concern emerges, in part, from the close association of rights with the law. My experience with the BC Civil Liberties Association is a reminder of the constant temptation to conflate human rights with the law. A sociological approach understands that human rights derive from society and the state rather than an abstract pre-social individual. Law, of course, has a long and essential association with rights. But there is a distinction between human rights laws, which are codified rules, and talking about human rights as aspirations or competing moral claims.[48] We should understand human rights as it is practised in social life.[49] Claims to universality confuse the way human rights are realized as a distinct social practice.[50] In this conversation, everyone has a voice because human rights are a product of human interaction, not legal reasoning.

My argument in the following essay essentially comes down to this: In defining human rights, we must first begin with those core rights that have always informed rights talk in Canada. This does not prevent the recognition of additional rights. But rather than insist that any grievance or injustice can be a human right, we should recognize that many contemporary rights claims might be better framed as social justice rather than human rights. This claim is rooted in a concern over the association between rights and the law, and law's inability to serve as a vehicle for pursuing transformative social change. In the subsequent essays, several leading scholars of human rights challenge my claim. Each is a leading expert in his or her field, and each was chosen for the purpose of critiquing the arguments in the main essay.

In "The Right Investment in Rights," Nathalie Des Rosiers rejects the dichotomy between law and social activism while at the same time embracing rights talk as empowering for those who are marginalized in our society. For Des Rosiers, concerns around rights inflation are exaggerated: "Rights evolution should not be thwarted by taxonomy debates that may counter and diminish meaningful political and legal advances for marginalized groups." She draws on her experiences as both a scholar and an activist, including as former General Counsel for the Canadian Civil Liberties Association and as the Dean of Common Law at the University of Ottawa. Another scholar and human rights practitioner, Pearl Eliadis, takes up this critique in "Too Many Rights?" She acknowledges that there has been a proliferation of rights in recent years, but rather than being concerned, she welcomes the recognition of new rights. She believes, as does Des Rosiers, that the law is a vehicle for social change. Too often, she points out, it is people with privilege and power who raise concerns around rights inflation. Instead of lamenting the widespread use of rights talk, particularly the way it has expanded the mandate of the courts and human rights law, she insists that these "findings show the adaptability of human rights, as well as their capacity to pull inchoate claims out of the chaos of their facts, and organize them into cogent claims for justice based on human rights principles." For Eliadis, what we are experiencing is not so much a rights *revolution* as a rights *evolution*.

Rhoda E. Howard-Hassmann has spent a career studying human rights activism, law, and politics in Canada and abroad. In "Liberalism, Social Democracy, and Human Rights," she questions the distinction between social justice and human rights. She envisions social democracy as an improvement on liberal democracy, in that it guarantees access to economic as well as civil and political human rights. Canadians, she argues, should not have to rely on charity to have enough to eat or go to school: "If human rights are historically contingent, then Canadian history has not stopped, and social movement actors are free to argue that there should be a human right to food ... If human rights are a social construction, then there is no reason why Canadian human rights law cannot extend beyond the core human rights of liberal democracy." Finally, Gert Verschraegen engages most directly with the sociology of human rights in "Historical Contingency and Human Rights Pluralism." Rather than criticizing the proliferation of rights, Verschraegen considers the dynamism, flexibility, and diversity of human rights as its great strength: "The language of human rights is attractive because it speaks to our individualism, enabling us to see ourselves as autonomous persons able to raise legal claims, yet it also connects us to a global 'imagined community' that provides us with the minimum recognition of abstract humanity." He rejects the notion of core rights on the basis that, if human rights are historically contingent, then it is impossible to identify a set of core rights fixed in time. Verschraegen addresses most directly a theme that is common among all the commentators' essays: that human rights are indivisible. Instead of seeing rights inflation as a problem, he has faith in the ability of political and legal institutions to filter the flood of emerging rights claims.

This book exemplifies an important debate around the implications of framing social problems as human rights violations. Some of the most prominent human rights scholars in the world, including Michael Ignatieff, James Griffin, Amy Gutman, and Eric Posner, have raised similar concerns about rights inflation and also make a case for core rights. The idea of rights inflation is understandably controversial. Rights talk is so pervasive today that most people instinctively use this language when they feel they have been treated unfairly. For a historical sociologist, however, there is nothing inevitable about human rights, nor is it strange to conceive of other ways of framing grievances. Moreover, it is evident that something profound has happened in recent history. It was rare, if not unprecedented, to read about a right to health care, information, or clean water in the past. This change entails more than what Hunt refers to as the unending rights revolution. For most of our history, rights inflation took the form of redefining long-standing principles such as free speech and equal treatment. Since the 1970s, however, there has been a growing tendency to frame an expansive range of grievances as human rights violations. Debating the meaning and implications of this change is the purpose of this book.

Notes

1 The Supreme Court of Nova Scotia ruled in 2015 that the legislation violated the right to free speech under the *Charter of Rights and Freedoms*. The legislation allows victims and their families to seek remedies through civil action in court, including protection or prevention orders. It defines cyberbullying as "any electronic communication through the use of technology including, without limiting the generality of the foregoing, computers, other electronic devices, social networks, text messaging, instant messaging, websites and electronic mail, typically repeated or with continuing effect, that is intended or ought reasonably be expected to cause fear, intimidation, humiliation, distress or other damage or harm to another person's health, emotional well-being, self-esteem or reputation, and includes assisting or encouraging such communication in any way." *An Act to Address and Prevent Cyberbullying*, Statutes of Nova Scotia, 2013, c.2; *Crouch v. Snell*, 2015 NSSC 340.

2 I use the term "due process" to refer to those rights listed in the *Canadian Charter of Rights and Freedoms* as "legal rights." Although the terminology is technically inappropriate—unlike in the United States, the term has no basis in constitutional law in Canada—I use it here because it is in common use in Canada.

3 For a history of human rights and Canada's rights culture, see Dominique Clément, *Human Rights in Canada: A History* (Waterloo: Wilfrid Laurier University Press, 2016).

4 Several historians argue that human rights did not become a common form of framing grievances until the 1970s. See, for instance, Jan Eckel and Samuel Moyn, eds., *The Breakthrough: Human Rights in the 1970s* (Philadelphia: University of Pennsylvania Press, 2014); Samual Moyn, *The Last Utopia: Human Rights in History* (Boston: Belknap Press of Harvard University Press, 2010). In political theory, although scholars developed theories of rights, they had yet to engage with the notion of human rights, as evinced by a bibliography of rights published in 1978 that did not use the term. John Rawls, in his famous book on theories of justice, did not use the term human rights. John Rawls, *A Theory of Justice* (New York: Oxford University Press, 1999); Moyn, *The Last Utopia*, 215.

5   Costas Douzinas, "The Poverty of (Rights) Jurisprudence," in *Human Rights Law*, ed. Connor Gearty and Costas Douzinas (Cambridge: Cambridge University Press, 2012), 56; William Black, 2002.

6   See, for instance, Gideon Sjoberg, Elizabeth A. Gill, and Norma Williams, "A Sociology of Human Rights," *Social Problems* 48, no. 1 (2001): 42.

7   Louis Henkin, *The Age of Rights* (New York: Columbia University Press, 1990).

8   Daniel Chong offers a formula for explaining how new human rights emerge in an international context. Daniel Chong, "Economic Rights and Extreme Poverty: Moving Towards Subsistence," in *The International Struggle for New Human Rights*, ed. Clifford Bob (Philadelphia: University of Pennsylvania Press, 2009).

9   Although international institutions facilitate agreements among nations on a set of universal abstract rights, there is an independent process by which our community determines the nature and implementation of rights in practice.

10   H.L.A. Hart, *Essays in Jurisprudence and Philosophy* (Oxford: Clarendon Press, 1983), 196–97.

11   Mirko Bagaric and James Allan, "The Vacuous Concept of Dignity," *Journal of Human Rights* 5, no. 2 (2006): 257.

12   Florian Hoffmann, "Foundations Beyond Law," in *Human Rights Law*, ed. Connor Gearty and Costas Douzinas (Cambridge: Cambridge University Press, 2012), 81.

13   Eric A. Posner, *The Twilight of Human Rights Law* (New York: Oxford University Press, 2014), 6.

14   Human rights have transformed how we understand the past. The failure to prevent human rights abuses in the past can be a powerful collective memory that mobilizes actors in the present. Memories of past abuse are recast as part of a "global narrative of human rights" abuses, which provides legitimacy in using contemporary institutions such as war crimes tribunals to punish past offenders. "These trials create legal precedents, which become customs, which in turn, can harden into law over time." Daniel Levy and Natan Sznaider, "Sovereignty Transformed: A Sociology of Human Rights," *British Journal of Sociology* 57, no. 4 (2006): 670.

15   Alan C. Cairns, "The Past and Future of the Canadian Administrative State," *University of Toronto Law Journal* 40, no. 1 (1990): 336–37.

16   "With industrial progress, one passes from the minimal code of rights of man to more elaborate rights. But progress should not blind us to the meaning of those minimal rights, for to assert them is to say that no society is so simple that its members can justly be denied them." Maurice Cranston, *What Are Human Rights?* (New York: Basic Books, 1973), 82.

17   "As the perceived usefulness of attaching the label "human right" to a given goal or value increases, it can be expected that a determined effort will be made by a wide range of special interest groups to locate their cause under the banner of human rights." Philip Alston, "Conjuring Up New Human Rights: A Proposal for Quality Control," *American Journal of International Law* 78, no. 3 (1984): 614.

18   Mary Ann Glendon, *Rights Talk: The Impoverishment of Political Discourse* (New York: Free Press, 1991), xi.

19   James Griffin, *On Human Rights* (New York: Oxford University Press, 2008), 92–93.

20   Michael Ignatieff, *Human Rights as Politics and Idolatry* (Princeton: Princeton University Press, 2001), x.

21   Posner, *The Twilight of Human Rights Law*, 94.

22   Conor Gearty, *Can Human Rights Survive?* (Cambridge: Cambridge University Press, 2006), 144.

23   "Some human rights, in, say, the social and political spheres, seem predicated upon the assumption that human agents must be able to acquire at least minimal economic necessities." Sjoberg, Gill, and Williams, "A Sociology of Human Rights," 43.

24   Rose Freedman and Jacob Mchangama suggest that human rights proliferation is apparent in the increasing number of treaties, resolutions, bodies, and institutions for human rights: "The proliferation of Special Procedure mandates raises questions of whether they strengthen human rights protection and promotion through increasing awareness and widening the scope of topics to be included under the umbrella of human rights, or if expansion weakens the system by diluting core rights, reducing resources available to mandate holders, and providing a smokescreen for states seeking to avoid scrutiny of their record on fundamental human rights." Rose Freedman and Jacob Mchangama, "Expanding or Diluting Human Rights?: The Proliferation of United Nations Special Procedures Mandates," *Human Rights Quarterly* 38, no. 1 (2016): 165.

25   Aryeh Neier, "Social and Economic Rights: A Critique," *Human Rights Brief* 13, no. 2 (2006).

26   Whereas some scholars, such as Jack Donnelly, insist that human rights are indivisible, others such as Henry Shue identify a set of basic rights that are those minimal expectations that human beings can require from others for survival and dignity. Henry Shue penned a well-known study in the 1990s suggesting that subsistence and physical security are "basic rights" from which all other rights derive. Henry Shue, *Basic Rights: Subsistence, Affluence and U.S. Foreign Policy* (Princeton: Princeton University Press, 1996). Jack Donnelly, *Universal Human Rights in Theory & Practice* (New York: Cornell University Press, 2003). On basic rights and rights inflation, see also Alan Gewirth, *The Community of Rights* (Chicago: University of Chicago Press, 1996), 101–5.

27   Michael Ignatieff, *Human Rights as Politics and Idolatry* (Princeton: Princeton University Press, 2001), 90.

28   For a critique of Ignatieff and minimalism, see Joshua Cohen, "Minimalism about Human Rights: The Most We Can Hope For?," *Journal of Political Philosophy* 12, no. 2 (2004).

29   Neier, "Social and Economic Rights."

30   Amartya Sen, *Development as Freedom* (New York: Random House, 2000). Similarly, John Rawls premised his theory of social justice on the idea that each person has equal basic liberties: "speech and assembly; liberty of conscience and freedom of thought; freedom of the person, which includes freedom from psychological oppression and physical assault and dismemberment (integrity of the person); the right to hold personal

property and freedom from arbitrary arrest and seizure as defined by the concept of the rule of law." Rawls, *A Theory of Justice*, 53.

31 Philip Alston, "A Framework for the Comparative Analysis of Bills of Rights," in *Promoting Human Rights through Bills of Rights: Comparative Perspectives*, ed. Philip Alston (New York: Oxford University Press, 1999), 2.

32 Brian Grodsky, "Weighing the Costs of Accountability: The Role of Institutional Incentives in Pursuing Transitional Justice," *Journal of Human Rights* 7, no. 4 (2008): 354.

33 Griffin, *On Human Rights*, 187, 92–93.

34 Mikael Rask Madsen and Gert Verschraegen, "Making Human Rights Intelligible: An Introduction to a Sociology of Human Rights," in *Making Human Rights Intelligible*, ed. Mikael Rask Madsen and Gert Verschraegen (Portland: Hart Publishing, 2013), 9. See also Patricia Hynes et al., "Sociology and Human Rights: Confrontations, Evasions and New Engagements," *International Journal of Human Rights* 14, no. 6 (2010).

35 I am also not challenging the notion of the indivisibility of human rights. Rather, I am suggesting that some grievances should not be framed as human rights violations.

36 Madsen and Verschraegen, "Making Human Rights Intelligible," 6.

37 Eckel and Moyn, *The Breakthrough*; Moyn, *The Last Utopia*; Clément, *Human Rights in Canada*.

38 Madsen and Verschraegen, "Making Human Rights Intelligible."

39 On the sociology of human rights, see Madsen and Verschraegen, "Making Human Rights Intelligible."

40 "Rights cannot be defined once and for all because their emotional basis continues to shift, in part in reaction to declarations of rights. Rights remain open to question because our sense of who has rights and what those rights are constantly changes. The human rights revolution is by definition unending." Lynn Hunt, *Inventing Human Rights: A History* (New York: W.W. Norton, 2007), 29.

41 "The French Revolution, more than any other event, revealed that human rights have their own inner logic. As the deputies faced the need to turn their lofty ideals into specific laws, they inadvertently developed a kind of conceivability or thinkability scale." When revolutionaries in eighteenth-century France acknowledged the legitimate claims of oppressed Protestants as consistent with the logic of their own *Declaration of the Rights of Man and of the Citizen*, Jews immediately sought to use the same logic to justify freedom for all religious minorities. And recognition of Jews' rights led women to demand the right to vote and own property. Hunt, *Inventing Human Rights*, 150.

42 Lawrence M. Friedman offers a few examples of how rights are historically contingent. Religious freedom, for instance, did not prevent England from prohibiting Catholics from sitting in Parliament until 1829. State constitutions in the United States included protections for free speech, which did not prevent those states from banning the publication of abolitionist literature in the nineteenth century. Lawrence M. Friedman, *The Human Rights Culture: A Study in History and Context* (New Orleans: Quid Pro Books, 2011), 26–28.

43   Madsen and Verschraegen, "Making Human Rights Intelligible," 2.

44   Ibid., 11.

45   Hart, *Essays in Jurisprudence and Philosophy*, 196–97; Bagaric and Allan, "The Vacuous Concept of Dignity," 257; Posner, *The Twilight of Human Rights Law*, 6.

46   As Amartya Sen argues, "the emergence of a shared recognition of that 'injustice' may be dependent in practice on open discussion of issues and feasibilities ... The role of public discussion to debate conventional wisdom on both practicalities and valuations can be central to the acknowledgement of injustice ... basic civil rights and political freedoms are indispensible for the emergence of social values. Indeed, the freedom to participate in critical evaluation and in the process of value formation is among the most crucial freedoms of societal existence." Sen, *Development as Freedom*, 287.

47   Charles R. Beitz, *The Idea of Human Rights* (New York: Oxford University Press, 2009), 142–43.

48   Richard Wilson distinguishes between human rights law and human rights talk: "the former refers to positivised rules in national and international law and the latter refers to how people speak about those norms, or aspire to expand or interpret them in new ways. Perhaps most importantly, this allows us to distinguish between written codes that have the backing of a coercive bureaucratic apparatus and those which may well not." Richard Ashby Wilson, "Tyrannosaurus Lex: The Anthropology of Human Rights and Transnational Law," in *The Practice of Human Rights: Tracking Law between the Global and the Local*, ed. Mark Goodale and Sally Engle Merry (Cambridge: Cambridge University Press, 2007), 350.

49   Griffin explores this point in greater detail: Griffin, *On Human Rights*, 29–30.

50   Jack Donnelly, a political scientist, has made a similar argument: "Such claims to historical or anthropological universality confuse values such as justice, fairness, and humanity with practices that aim to realize those values. Rights—entitlements that ground claims with a special force—are a particular kind of social practice. Human rights—equal and inalienable entitlements of all individuals that may be exercised against the state and society—are a distinctive way to seek to realize social values such as justice and human flourishing. There may be considerable historical/anthropological universality of values across time and culture. No society, civilization, or culture prior to the seventeenth century, however, had a widely endorsed practice, or even vision, of equal and inalienable individual human rights." Jack Donnelly, "The Relative Universality of Human Rights," *Human Rights Quarterly* 29, no. 2 (2007): 284.

Rights Inflation in Canada

One of the most difficult lessons to teach about human rights is that we have not always framed our grievances using the language of rights. In the past, Canadians were more likely to reference socialism, industrial democracy, Christian values, or British justice when they felt wronged and sought restitution. When the Chinese Consolidated Benevolent Association mobilized a campaign against segregated schools in 1923, for instance, they argued that "segregation is contrary to all British Ideals of Justice [and] Fair Play."[1] Among the most vocal advocates for a bill of rights by the mid-twentieth century were leaders of the Co-Operative Commonwealth Federation, many of whom insisted that racism was contrary to Christian principles.[2]

The earliest and most visible campaigns for rights in Canadian history were a response to state repression in colonies. The Conquest of 1759 introduced British legal traditions, including the Magna Carta (1215), habeas corpus (1679), and the Bill of Rights (1689). But the colonies were ruled by a series of autocratic British governors who had little patience for civil liberties. They jailed journalists and closed newspapers. Catholics faced widespread restrictions, especially in holding public office. It is hardly surprising, therefore, that colonists demanded civil and political rights as well as responsible government. Reformers, including those who led the failed rebellions in 1837–38, defined rights in this period in terms of speech, association, assembly, press, religion, equal treatment, and due process. The republicans who drafted Lower Canada's 92

Resolutions, which became a·manifesto for the *Patriotes*, talked about freedom of religion and due process of law. Robert Nelson, one of the *Patriote* leaders, issued a Declaration of Independence in 1838 that made reference to religious freedom, free speech, and trial by jury as well as the right to vote. William Lyon Mackenzie, the leader of Upper Canada's resistance, drafted another constitution that recognized "civil and religious liberty" and provided guarantees against excessive bail and cruel and unusual punishment. But none of them spoke of *human* rights. Citizenship was a precondition to having rights. Reformers anchored their conception of rights to British legal tradition and appealed to notions of British justice.[3] Moreover, some reformers demanded equal treatment for Catholics but refused to support equal rights for women or minorities.

A similar discourse around rights informed the Confederation debates in the 1860s. One of the foundations of Confederation was the principle of equal treatment for Catholics and Protestants. The constitution guaranteed certain rights for French and English Canadians, as well as the right to operate Catholic or Protestant schools. It also required periodic elections. But Confederation, as Janet Ajzestat argues, did not fundamentally challenge how Canadians talked about rights.[4] There was no bill of rights in the constitution. Canadians placed their faith in Parliament to protect rights. Similarly, at the time in the country's leading English-language newspapers, the *Globe and Mail* (or its predecessor, *The Globe*) and the *Winnipeg Free Press*—rights talk was still framed in terms of British justice (or civil liberties). Between 1844 and 1870, as well as in 1892 and 1897, only a few dozen articles used the term civil liberties (rarely human rights).[5] Most of these articles discussed religious freedom, especially denominational education.

Public debates surrounding rights rose to prominence during the First and Second World Wars. The federal government suspended habeas corpus; imposed widespread censorship; declared numerous associations to be unlawful; broke strikes and banned newspapers from reporting on them (and later banned striking); restricted due process to facilitate prosecutions; interned thousands of "enemy aliens"; and imposed conscription, which led to the jailing of thousands of men for desertion. Yet in debates around the government's wartime policies in Parliament, in the media, and by advocacy groups, the term "human rights" was rarely used.

By the mid-twentieth century, Canadians' rights vernacular had changed little. This was especially evident during Parliamentary hearings around a possible federal bill of rights held in 1947, 1948, and 1950.[6] Parliamentarians and community organizations had a narrow conception of rights, one that did, however, encompass speech, association, assembly, press, religion, equal treatment, and due process.[7] Similarly, the country's major newspapers continued to frame rights issues during this period as civil liberties. The two papers printed a combined six hundred articles on civil liberties or human rights between the years 1910 to 1915 and 1937 to 1939. The term human rights was only beginning to enter the print media's vernacular by the mid-twentieth century: 15 to 20 percent of the articles employed this term.[8] In most cases, the issue under discussion was due process, democracy, restrictions on free speech and the right to assemble (e.g., for communists or unionists), property rights, or the right of workers to organize and strike.

By the mid-twentieth century a profound shift was under way: Canadians were increasingly associating rights with a universal principle rather than British justice. The most notable aspect of this shift was that it acknowledged the widespread practice of discrimination. There had been prominent debates in the past surrounding discrimination against Catholics, for instance, but discrimination against women and minorities had gained greater prominence by the mid-twentieth century. People were now successfully appropriating rights discourse to demand equal treatment. Between 1962 and 1979 Canada developed the most sophisticated human rights legal system in the world: it was more expansive, accessible, and better enforced than any other.[9] But it was also rooted in the same tradition of rights that had long dominated rights talk in Canada. Saskatchewan's pioneering Bill of Rights (1947) recognized such rights as free speech, assembly, religion, association, and due process while at the same time prohibiting discrimination on the basis of race, religion, or national origin. The scope of human rights statutes in Canada expanded dramatically over the following years, but they remained primarily concerned with the principle of equal treatment and with prohibiting discrimination.

Nonetheless, this period was a pivotal moment in the history of rights in Canada.[10] Historian Samuel Moyn maintains that human rights in its current form dates not to the Enlightenment but to the 1970s.[11] In Canada, only by then were people speaking of rights more and more as "human rights" rather than "civil liberties." For the first time in Canada's history, the country's major newspapers were framing rights violations more often as human rights than as civil liberties. In 1976 and 1977 the *Globe and Mail* and the *Winnipeg Free Press* printed more than one thousand articles documenting human rights violations in Canada. Moreover, the range of issues that were being discussed in terms of rights was far broader than in the past. They included disability; housing; privacy; work; due process; immigration; discrimination; police powers; hate speech; censorship; children; lesbians and gays; language rights; and many others. The rights revolution was apparent in many other ways. Human rights were becoming a component of foreign policy. Canada signed numerous international human rights treaties and imposed sanctions on other countries—for example, it voted to expel South Africa from the Commonwealth.[12] It also became common in political debates to frame grievances as human rights violations.[13]

Social movements, in particular, wholeheartedly embraced human rights as a vision for social change. For example, the Canadian Association for Community Living, which was founded in 1958 as a family-oriented community living organization for people with disabilities, had become increasingly rights-conscious by the 1970s. In fact, the entire movement for people with disabilities underwent a transformation: advocacy had once been focused on social security, health policy, or welfare; now, a new generation was framing their grievances in terms of human rights and equality.[14] Disability rights associations proliferated, and traditional consumer organizations were increasingly framing their grievances as human rights violations.[15] Similar developments transformed social movements advocating for women, gays and lesbians, civil liberties, and many other issues.[16]

The trend towards framing grievances as human rights was best exemplified in the hearings of Parliament's Special Joint Committee on the Constitution in 1981–82, which eventually produced the *Charter of Rights and Freedoms*. At no other time in Canadian history had the state engaged in such an expansive consultation with Canadians about human rights. Organizations representing people with disabilities, Aboriginal peoples, women, children, racial minorities, ethnic minorities, prisoners, religions, people living in poverty, sexual minorities, and workers participated in the consultations. They demanded recognition for a broad range of grievances related to language, learning, health care, education, the minimum wage, self-determination, rest and leisure, meaningful work, abortion, day care, mobility, family reunification, cultural retention, and much more. It was not simply that such demands were being forwarded—women had been campaigning for publicly funded child care for generations—but that people were now articulating these grievances in the language of human rights.

The popularizing of human rights has transformed rights talk in Canada. From the rebellions of the 1830s through to Confederation, the two world wars, and the era of constitutional reform, public debates around rights had been dominated by a narrow conception of rights that included political freedoms (speech, association, assembly, press), the right to vote, religious freedom, equal treatment, and due process. Canada's embrace of human rights discourse has facilitated the emergence of new rights claims. References to British justice or civil liberties had been associated with citizenship and civil and political freedoms; human rights is a universal principle that today encompasses a much broader range of rights. As Moyn argues, "there is a clear and fundamental difference between earlier rights, all predicated on belonging to a political community, and eventual 'human rights.' If so, the droits de l'homme that powered early modern revolution and nineteenth-century politics need to be rigorously distinguished from the 'human rights' coined in the 1940s that have grown so appealing in the last few decades."[17]

Core rights are those rights that have always informed public discourse in Canada. To be sure, Canadians have mobilized around poverty for as long as they have mobilized to protect free speech. But only since the 1970s has it become common to frame such grievances as human rights violations. Meanwhile, the meaning and application of core rights is constantly being debated.

Many of the most prominent debates around rights in Canadian history involved freedom of religion. Throughout the nineteenth century, it was not uncommon to see Protestants and Catholics battling on the streets of Toronto or Halifax. Confederation was made possible by an agreement to guarantee both Protestants and Catholics the right to religious education. Denominational education was among the most divisive issues in Canada for many decades and was often framed as a question of minority rights. Distaste for religious minorities, including Hutterites, Doukhobors, and Jehovah's Witnesses, resulted in some of the most oppressive laws in twentieth-century Canada.[18] Similarly, free speech has long been a contested right. French and British governors jailed journalists and politicians who criticized the regime. In 1810, Chief Justice Sewell of Lower Canada explained to the grand jury in the *Le Canadien* case that freedom of the press did not mean the right to criticize the government.[19] During the First and Second World Wars, anyone who criticized the war effort could be interned or sent to jail. In the 1930s the government of Alberta tried to explicitly censor the press by requiring newspapers to file stories with the government before they were published (the law was overturned in court). In the same way, due process has always been a contested right, from the suspension of habeas corpus during the American and French Revolutions to the Fenian Raids, wartime policy, the October Crisis, and the current war on terror. The Cold War produced an extensive security apparatus that included surveillance and security screening programs. Civil servants, immigrants, refugees, defence contractors, and others were carefully screened, and many were denied employment with no right of appeal. Communists were tried and convicted for sedition. By the 1970s, the RCMP alone had files on more than 800,000 Canadians.[20]

In some ways, little has changed: Canadians continue to struggle over the meaning and scope of freedom of religion.[21] When a retired lawyer in Ontario attempted to create an Islamic Institute of Civil Justice in 2003 to provide private arbitration based on *sharia* law, his effort ignited a nationwide debate. The Ontario government quickly amended the *Arbitration Act* to prohibit the use of religious practices in arbitrations (which had the effect of placing restrictions on Jewish people who had already been using religious courts). In 2006 the Supreme Court of Canada ruled that a Sikh's freedom of religion had been violated when a public school forbade a young man to carry a *kirpan* (ceremonial dagger). In Bountiful, British Columbia, a polygamist sect had insisted that the practice of marrying multiple young girls to one man—and the resulting high rates of teen pregnancy, isolation, and lower educational achievement for women—was protected as a religious freedom. However, in 2011 the BC Supreme Court upheld the *Criminal Code* provision prohibiting polygamy. A group called Secular Ontario filed several lawsuits against city councils in 2012 to ban the opening of council meetings with the Lord's Prayer.[22] In 2013 a woman filed a complaint with the Ontario Human Rights Commission when a Muslim barber refused to cut her hair because he served only men.[23] Trinity Western University, a private evangelical Christian institution based in Vancouver, sparked a controversy in 2001 when it sought to establish a teacher training program. The Supreme Court of Canada ordered the BC College of Teachers to approve the teaching program despite the university's requirement that professors and students sign a pledge to not engage in premarital sex or homosexual relationships.[24] That issue returned to the spotlight in 2014 when the province tentatively approved a law school for TWU. Law societies in Ontario, Nova Scotia, and BC voted to reject accreditation for any TWU graduate.[25] The Supreme Court ultimately sided with the law societies in 2018 on the basis that it was "proportionate and reasonable" to limit religious rights to protect equality rights.[26]

Religious freedom remains highly contested in Canada. There is an ongoing debate over whether the state should require marriage officiates to marry same-sex couples, and whether doctors and pharmacists must provide treatments and medications when doing so would violate their religious beliefs. Several recent cases have highlighted the conflict between religious beliefs and the rights of gays and lesbians: a printer denied a request to produce letterhead for a gay rights organization; the Knights of Columbus refused to rent a hall for a lesbian marriage; and a young man wanted to bring his boyfriend to the prom at a Catholic school.[27] The rising visibility of burqas and niqabs (a full-face veil) has led a few European countries to impose dress codes in public schools as well as restrictive immigration policies. France and Belgium have gone so far as to ban wearing the burqa in public, and the former has passed a Charter of Secularism to restrict expressions of religious belief in schools.[28] In 2016, several French cities even banned the burkini—a swimsuit worn by some Muslim women (images of French police ordering women to remove clothing on beaches quickly gained international headlines).[29] In contrast, Canadian authorities have sought greater accommodation for religious minorities. Canadian courts are more likely to insist that employers and public institutions accommodate religious observances. The Federal Court, for example, has affirmed that Mounties have the right to wear a turban as part of their uniform. The Supreme Court of Canada ruled in 2013 that judges had to offer latitude to women who wished to wear a niqab when appearing as witnesses in court.[30] Nonetheless, Canadian courts have allowed equality rights to trump religious minority rights in most cases.[31] In 2013, the Parti Québécois government proposed a Charter of Quebec Values that would have banned religious symbols for all public officials and institutions (with minor exemptions). The proposal bitterly divided the province and was immensely controversial.[32] Minority rights claims, especially when they are perceived as restricting women's equality or as discriminating against sexual minorities, will remain a divisive human rights issue for future generations.[33]

As with religion, for most of our history Canadians have grappled over the scope of free speech.[34] It is ironic, then, that free speech has become the rallying cry in recent years to justify vicious attacks on minorities. In Regina, Bill Whatcott spent much of 2001 walking up to people's homes and stuffing flyers into mailboxes depicting homosexuals as sodomites who were a threat to children. Meanwhile, the *Red Deer Advocate* was publishing Reverend Stephen Boissoin's letters to the editor that condemned homosexuality as wicked and dangerous and compared gays to pedophiles, pimps, and drug dealers. Between 2005 and 2007, *Maclean's* magazine published a series of articles that were critical of Islam and Muslims. Columnist Barbara Amiel bemoaned immigration from Arab countries while Mark Steyn warned that Muslim youths would undermine Western society. Both columnists' disdain for Muslims, which included inferences about raping minors and bestiality in Iran, led them to warn Canadians that their society and way of life was in danger.[35] Human rights complaints were filed in each case. But Amiel, Steyn, and Whatcott insisted that human rights statutes' hate speech provisions violated their right to free speech. Ernst Zundel, a holocaust denier, and James Keegstra, who taught anti-Semitism to his high school students, had both used this same defence when they were prosecuted under the *Criminal Code* in the 1990s (Zundel under the false news section, Keegstra under the hate propaganda section).[36]

Free speech has become one of the most divisive human rights issues in Canada. According to Richard Moon, a law professor who was hired in 2008 to assess the hate speech provisions of the *Canadian Human Rights Act*, hate speech is an especially contentious issue for two reasons: hate speech complaints have targeted individuals who are expressing ideas that reflect more widely held views, and they have been filed against mainstream publications such as *Maclean's*.[37] The results have been mixed. The cases against *Maclean's*, Boissoin, and Zundel failed (in the latter case, the Supreme Court of Canada struck down the false news section), whereas Whatcott's and Keegstra's convictions were upheld.

These cases highlight the tension around our free speech: there have always been limits on speech, which begets the questions of how far we can tolerate hateful speech before it becomes dangerous. Canada was one of the first countries to criminalize hate speech, which now includes speech aimed at sexual orientation. Yet politicians, journalists, lawyers, and advocacy groups continue to stoke debate on this issue.[38] The media, in particular, has largely opposed hate speech laws. Out of 126 editorials and opinion columns published in a dozen newspapers between 2006 and 2013—including *Maclean's*, the *Toronto Star*, the *National Post*, and the *Globe and Mail*—94 called for the repeal of hate speech provisions in human rights statutes. In almost every case, the newspaper's formal editorial position was to repeal the laws.[39] The divisive nature of this issue has created a situation where hate speech violates human rights law in only a few provinces (while it is a criminal offence across the country).

Due process also has a long and contentious history in Canada. This is especially apparent in governments' willingness to restrict rights during periods of perceived crisis or in response to internal and external threats.[40] Our post-9/11 response has been largely consistent with past practices. The *Anti-Terrorism Act* gives police the power to detain suspected terrorists for three days without charge and to compel them to answer questions in a secret hearing.[41] That law creates several new terrorism-related offences with strict penalties; allows for greater electronic surveillance of Canadian citizens; criminalizes motive—a rarity in Canadian law—by defining terrorism as seeking to advance political, religious, or ideological causes; and empowers the government to ban or revoke the charitable status of any organization that supports terrorists at home or abroad.[42] Highly controversial amendments to the Act in 2015 introduced an unprecedented new power—to "disrupt" potential terrorist activities—without a clear definition of those activities or proper oversight. The amendments further expanded the police's powers of preventative detention as well as their power to collect information on citizens.[43] Similarly, the *Immigration Act* has provisions for security certificates, which have been used to issue warrants to deport non-citizens out of fear that they are potential terrorists.[44]

Twenty-seven such certificates were issued between 1991 and 2006; five of these individuals were held indefinitely because they could not be deported to countries where they might be tortured. It is a hallmark of every democracy that no individual can be imprisoned by the state without due process, yet Hassan Almrei was imprisoned for eight years in Canada without charge. And as Canadians discovered in 2013, our government has mimicked the Americans in using new technologies to create a system for gathering vast amounts of private data on its own citizens.[45]

At the same time, though, Canada's rights revolution has produced a culture that is sensitive to restrictions on due process. The government faces a much higher burden for demonstrating the need for extreme measures today than it did in 1939. The *War Measures Act*, for instance, was replaced in 1988 with the *Emergencies Act*. Unlike its predecessor, which was little more than a two-page statute that allowed the federal cabinet to rule the country by decree, the new legislation offers a more precise definition of an emergency; places restrictions on when emergency powers are warranted; requires Parliamentary approval; and empowers Parliament to revoke the declaration of any orders issued under the law.[46] Similarly, the *Anti-Terrorism Act* has stronger provisions to protect human rights than comparable legislation in other countries: a sunset clause on preventative arrests and investigative hearings; a shorter period of preventative detention; a prohibition on using compelled testimony in criminal proceedings; exemptions for protests and strikes; exclusion of speech as sufficient cause for proving terrorists' motives; not criminalizing membership in a terrorist organization; and provisions for external oversight on intelligence gathering.[47] In 2007 the Supreme Court of Canada ordered the federal government to hire special legal advocates who could cross-examine the evidence underlying a security certificate (albeit without disclosing that information to the detainee).[48]

Religion, speech, and due process are only a few examples of how some rights have always been integral to rights talk in Canada and of how rights are historically contingent in that they are shaped by their historical context. In 2003, Canadians were split over whether forbidding civil marriage for same-sex couples was similar to discrimination against people of colour or women.[49] Two years later a similar poll found that, although a majority of Canadians supported gay rights, 60 percent still wanted to define marriage as a union between one man and one woman.[50] However, by 2010, 68 percent of Canadians supported a change in the legal definition of marriage, and in 2011, 70 percent of Albertans supported the right to same-sex marriage.[51] When asked about abortion in 2010, a majority of Canadians (73 percent) agreed that it was a personal right although only 55 percent of respondents believed "there is no point in re-opening the debate."[52] Fifty-seven percent of respondents in a 2010 poll stated that Canada has a long way to go to achieve full gender equality.[53] People were asked in 2000 about the likelihood of there being reduced prejudice against ethnic and racial minorities in Canada over the next decade: only 67 percent indicated that this was either very likely or somewhat likely to occur.[54] In 2011, however, 74 percent of respondents agreed with the statement that Canadian society had become less tolerant of others since 9/11, while 60 percent believed that Muslims in Canada were discriminated against more than before.[55] In addition, 59 percent of respondents attributed a "negative impression of certain ethnicities and religious faiths" to the 9/11 attacks.[56]

There are virtually no limits to how people employ rights talk today, from the most profound violations of individual freedom to the most mundane realities of daily life. The *Universal Declaration of Human Rights* recognized a few dozen rights when it was enacted in 1948. Today, international treaties recognize more than three hundred human rights.[57] These rights range from free speech and religion to the right to housing, food, and health care and the right to live independently or within a community. Several countries and international organizations have recognized security, a healthy environment, and peace as human rights.[58] Since 2002, many countries have celebrated International Right to Know Day to promote freedom of information. There is also growing support to recognize a "right to development," which asserts a duty on wealthy countries to transfer resources to raise the standard of living in poorer nations. South Africa's constitution includes rights to adequate housing, food and water, health care, and social security.[59] Croatia's constitution recognizes the right to health care, a healthy environment, and a healthy life.[60] A recent history of the Olympic movement talks about the "right to the city." The authors argue that security zones, such as those that were created for the Vancouver 2010 Olympics, violate the right to access streets, shopping malls, and riverfronts.[61] Since the proliferation of freedom of information statutes around the world in the 1980s, including every jurisdiction in Canada, at least forty-two nations have enshrined the right to obtain government information in their constitution.[62] This has led at least one judge in Canada to suggest that there is a "right to the preservation of Canada's documentary heritage."[63] It is not uncommon to hear Canadians speak today of clean water, assisted suicide, and natural resources as human rights.

One aspect of rights inflation involves revisiting and reinterpreting rights. This is an essential and healthy form of rights inflation. The Supreme Court of Canada ruled in 1987 that the *Charter of Rights and Freedoms*' guarantee of freedom of association did not apply to collective bargaining. Labour rights, according to the Court, were modern rights that had been excluded from the new constitution. In 2007, however, the Court overturned its previous ruling. To justify its decision, the judges had to reinterpret the history of labour relations in Canada. They argued that labour rights predated the constitution and were not the creation of contemporary labour relations.[64] As it turns out, this was only the beginning. In a landmark decision in 2015 the Supreme Court of Canada created a right to strike. The Court struck down Saskatchewan's labour legislation declaring all public sector workers as potential essential services; it also decreed that unnecessary restrictions on labour's right to strike violated freedom of association.[65]

This was not the first time the Supreme Court of Canada had created a right after declaring, years earlier, that no such right existed. In a stunning decision handed down in December 2013, the

Court declared that the country's solicitation laws were inconsistent with the *Charter of Rights and Freedoms*. It is hard to imagine a more striking example of rights inflation than a court overturning criminal laws that have existed since before Confederation. The Court has, in essence, created a new right in declaring that the *Criminal Code* provisions restricting solicitation infringe on the "rights of prostitutes by depriving them of security of the person in a manner that is not in accordance with the principles of fundamental justice."[66] Two years later, the Court struck down the criminal prohibition on assisted suicide as a violation of the right to physical security after having ruled years earlier that it was not a right.[67]

Another example of this type of rights inflation is the way that conservatives have enthusiastically embraced rights discourse.[68] Human rights, by the 1970s, were largely associated with left activism and politics. For instance, as late as the 1980s no conservative government among Western nations linked human rights with foreign policy.[69] Since the 1980s, however, conservatives have cultivated an alternative doctrine of human rights that rejects liberal internationalism (law) in favour of a more ideologically (morally) oriented rights frame.[70] Similarly, it is now common for conservatives to frame their tough-on-crime stance in the form of a victims' bill of rights; opposition to abortion as the right to life; hate speech against minorities as a right to free speech; and military intervention abroad as promoting democratic rights.[71] Even this form of rights inflation is helpful. It sustains a constructive debate around our rights culture. It demonstrates that rights are never secure.

Clearly, then, rights are not immutable. Human rights are continually adapting as times change. It is a social process involving the emergence of new claims premised on human rights principles. Sometimes this acceptance takes the form of law. In 2012, for example, a woman in her mid-twenties argued before the British Columbia Court of Appeal that the prohibition on sex discrimination in the form of sexual harassment should be extended to accommodation. She won $10,000 in compensation against a landlord who was constantly making sexual advances and touching her inappropriately.[72] Human rights progress, though, entails a dialogue. Rights inflation challenges the boundaries of our rights culture through rights claims that offer a new understanding of rights. Is text messaging, for instance, free speech? When same-sex marriage was legalized in Canada in 2005, many people asserted the right to refuse to marry same-sex couples by appealing to freedom of religion. In this way, rights inflation contributes to maintaining a healthy dialogue about rights as society changes.

It is surprising how, more than a generation after the first human rights laws were enacted, discrimination remains such a prevalent social problem. A 2011 study titled "Why Do Some Employers Prefer to Interview Matthew, but Not Samir," involved sending seven thousand fake resumés to employers in Vancouver, Montreal, and Toronto. The authors found that employers in Canada's most diverse cities were 40 percent more likely to interview applicants with English-sounding names despite equal education, skills, and work histories (employers also weed out immigrants by requiring "Canadian experience").[73] A UBC study found that landlords were more likely to discriminate against homosexuals and single parents. This was precisely the case when a gay couple in Grand Forks, BC, arrived at a local bed and breakfast and was refused accommodation because of the owner's religious beliefs. The owner was found guilty of violation the provincial *Human Rights Act* in 2012 and fined.[74] Another study, this one by Quebec's human rights commission, published in 2011, found that temporary foreign workers routinely experienced discrimination because of their race, language, gender, and ethnic or national origin.[75] Soon after the report was published, temporary foreign workers employed at a Tim Hortons submitted a human rights complaint claiming that they had been subjected to racist comments and forced to work in worse conditions than other employees.[76] In 2014 the BC Human Rights Tribunal awarded a record-breaking $600,000 to fifty-five tree planters who had to deal with racial slurs, lower pay, and poor working conditions because of their race. (The government shut down the camp after workers complained that they had not eaten in two days.)[77] Frustrated with the lack of access to washrooms at restaurants, a group of people with disabilities in Nova Scotia banded together in 2018 to pressure the human rights commission to demand that the government enforce its own regulations.[78]

In December 2006 the federal government reduced the budget of the Status of Women Canada program by nearly 25 percent and eliminated twelve of sixteen of its regional offices. The *Globe and Mail*, among other newspapers, insisted that this was a wise decision: "The world was far different when the agency was established in the early 1970s ... Today, it seems more like a government relic, laden with jargon from old wars."[79] In 2013 the *National Post* echoed these comments when a columnist insisted that "racism, sexism and homophobia have become rare in Canadian public life."[80] Yet the idea that gender equality is no longer a social problem seems absurd, given the prevalence of female job ghettos, lower pay, underrepresentation in business and politics, and the feminization of poverty (especially for unmarried women with young children).[81] A generation after securing the right to not be fired for being pregnant, human rights tribunals continue to find people guilty: the BC Human Rights Coalition reported a rise in pregnancy discrimination cases in 2010–11 (21 of 165 cases); 25 percent of the Alberta Human Rights Commission's 2,138 complaints in 2009–10 involved pregnancy; and human rights commissions in Saskatchewan and Manitoba also noted large increases since 2009.[82] Many other forms of discrimination remain common. Landlords continue to be fined for refusing to rent to same-sex couples.[83] The Ontario Human Rights Commission ruled that a bottling company discriminated against a woman with a mental disability when it paid her only $1.25 per hour while paying non-disabled workers the minimum wage.[84] Quebec's human rights commission produced a report in 2011 citing concerns around the continuing practice of racial profiling among police.[85] And in 2015 the Human Rights Tribunal of Ontario handed down record-setting awards of $150,000 and $100,000 respectively to two female temporary foreign workers from Mexico who had been harassed and pressured into providing sexual favours to their employer.[86]

Meanwhile, technology is forcing us to update our thinking about rights. After Lisa McIntosh ended a relationship with her boss, Zbigniew Augustynowicz, at Metro Aluminum Products, he began harassing her by "sexting" her at work. McIntosh repeatedly demanded to be left alone, but he continued to send her messages requesting sexual favours from her and her daughter. The BC Human Rights Tribunal awarded McIntosh almost $30,000 in 2011 for Augustynowicz's "textual harassment."[87] A similar case in Ontario in 2012 demonstrated how technology is the new frontier for sex discrimination. S.S. worked as a waitress at Marshy's Bar-B-Que & Grill in Ottawa from September 2008 to February 2009.[88] After making several comments about her breasts in front of co-workers, the manager, Quinton Taylor, began leaving crude text messages and voicemails on her cellphone while at a party with her co-workers. The harassment continued to the point that S.S. had to quit and seek psychiatric help. The Ontario Human Rights Commission awarded her $15,000.[89] There have also been cases around whether death threats on Facebook should be considered free speech or a criminal offence.[90]

Many of the human rights controversies that have emerged in recent years can be unsettling because they suggest new ways of thinking about rights, especially equal treatment. Female ski jumpers, for instance, filed a human rights complaint in 2008 because the Olympics banned women from participating in that sport.[91] More recently, in 2014, female soccer players alleged that forcing women to play on artificial turf in the upcoming 2015 World Cup in Canada was discriminatory because they would be more likely to suffer injuries.[92] The Quebec Human Rights Commission ruled against a Muslim woman who insisted that she be served by a woman when required to remove her niqab to have a photograph taken for her health card. In another case, the commission determined that people could not refuse service from a health board employee because she was wearing a hijab.[93] Ninety-two-year-old Denis Olorenshaw launched a human rights complaint in 2012 when Western Assurance quoted him a higher premium for car insurance than his sixty-two-year-old daughter.[94] At the Great Blue Heron Charity Casino in Port Perry, a part-time employee pursued a five-year human rights complaint after she was refused a full-time job. She claimed that the company's policy of restricting staff to cleaning bathrooms of their own gender was sex discrimination after the casino had replaced a male employee with another man (she was awarded back pay and $10,000).[95] Guy Earle, a volunteer master of ceremonies for an open-mike comedy night at Zesty's restaurant, was accused of discrimination on the basis of sexual orientation in 2007 when he started yelling profanities at a lesbian couple during the show and called them "dykes." He was found guilty and the couple was awarded $22,000 in damages.[96] Several other human rights complaints involving restaurants were brought in 2016 from women who argued that a requirement to wear revealing clothes created an environment conducive to sexual harassment.[97]

Human rights commissions have become sites of contestation over the meaning of human rights. Ted Kindos, the owner of Gator Ted's Tap & Grill in Burlington, had to pay $10,000 in damages after kicking out a man who was smoking marijuana in the doorway. The Ontario Human Rights Commission determined that he was guilty of discrimination on the basis of disability because the marijuana was medicinal.[98] In another case, a woman was fired from her job after her boss complained that her lunch food smelled (she was heating curry in the microwave) and that her religious clothing was unprofessional. A human rights tribunal ruled that the company's dress code was discriminatory, as was its microwave policy. It ordered the employer to pay $36,000 in damages and take sensitivity training.[99] "Big Mike," a 430-pound man who was in prison for drug trafficking, convinced the Quebec human rights commission to award him $10,000 from the Public Security Ministry because it failed to reasonably accommodate his size.[100] Quebec's human rights commission awarded $8,000 to a Montreal panhandler—sixty-three-year-old Francine Beaumont—who routinely solicited customers outside a liquor store. Robert Delisle was found guilty of discrimination on the basis of social status for writing an offensive letter to the liquor store about killing Beaumont, which the store printed and showed her.[101] Medical researchers and activists filed an injunction in 2014 against the federal government's restrictions on prescribing heroin. They insisted that, for the small number of addicts who do not benefit from methadone treatments, the federal government's refusal to allow doctors to prescribe narcotics violated their right to physical security and discriminated on the basis of addiction.[102] Perhaps the most controversial and difficult discrimination cases, though, involve family status. A federal human rights tribunal ordered a government department to reimburse an employee $17,000 in 2014 to cover the cost of retaining two separate residences following a relocation from Nova Scotia to Ontario. In this case, the employee's wife had remained in the original residence to care for his ailing mother.[103] A more recent case, in 2018, involved a mother arguing before a human rights commission that an employer should not be allowed to change her shifts because she needed to start worker later in the day so that she could drop her child off at child care.[104] There have been other cases requiring employers to accommodate child care needs, for example, by adjusting shift work and allowing employees to refuse to relocate away from family.

The existence of human rights laws and commissions facilitates rights inflation. Such laws encourage individuals to frame their grievances using the language of rights. Citizens for Safe Technology argued before a human rights tribunal that BC Hydro's smart meters discriminated on the basis of disability because some people are hypersensitive to electromagnetic technology.[105] A group of seven women filed an age discrimination complaint when InStore, which hires women to display food in grocery stores, fired them because they did not look like "soccer moms."[106] The BC–Yukon Association of Drug Warrior Survivors brought a complaint before the provincial human rights commission against the City of Abbotsford for a 2005 bylaw blocking access to sterile needle exchange facilities and supervised injection sites; the group claimed that the bylaw violated the rights of drug users.[107] The municipality of Iroquois Falls in Ontario had to fend off a human rights complaint that sought to stretch the definition of discrimination on the basis of disability to force municipalities to clear snow piled up in front of the driveways of disabled homeowners.[108] Ontario's Human Rights Commission argued in 2015 before the tribunal that the Toronto

Police Service's refusal to recognize on the memorial wall those offi-
cers who died while on duty as a result of suicide linked to mental
illness was employment-based discrimination.[109] All of these cases
have at least one common quality: they challenge our traditional
notions of discrimination and equal treatment.[110]

Rights inflation also takes the form of advancing entirely new rights
claims. Since the popularization of human rights as a way of framing grievances, rights inflation has taken on a new life. No less than
Canada's oldest and largest human rights commission declared in
2018 that poverty was a human rights violation and would, therefore, be a priority for Ontario's commission in the future.[111] Framing systemic social problems such as environmental degradation
and poverty as rights violations is not the same as reinterpreting
core rights. Problems like these represent an entirely new class of
human rights claims. It is increasingly unclear what distinguishes a
rights violation from other grievances.

Without in any way judging the validity of new rights claims,
it is apparent that human rights are how people now frame almost
any type of grievance. In 2012 the Ontario Human Rights Commission suggested that requiring a job applicant to reveal his or
her Facebook password might be a human rights violation.[112]
That same year, the chief content officer for Netflix was quoted in
Forbes as saying that Canada's low broadband caps and high access
fees are a human rights violation.[113] The Yukon Human Rights
Commission and numerous advocacy groups—including the Pivot
Legal Society and Canada Without Poverty—are seeking recognition of a human right to housing.[114] Even the Prime Minister of
Canada vowed in 2017 to recognize housing as a human right.[115]
Unions routinely refer to back-to-work legislation as a violation
of labour's human rights. In fact, the Saskatchewan Federation of
Labour argued before the Supreme Court of Canada that "the right
to withdraw labour is a universal human right."[116] In 2013 the
leader of the Liberal Party in Manitoba introduced a private members' bill that would have added bullying to the provincial human

rights code.[117] The right to clean air, water, food, and land has also garnered headlines in recent years.[118] In 2010 the United Nations formally recognized a human right to water and sanitation.

One of the most controversial human rights decisions in recent years involved an assertion of Aboriginal rights under the *Charter of Rights and Freedoms*. An Ontario judge ruled in 2014 that Aboriginal peoples had a "constitutionally protected right to pursue their traditional medicine."[119] As a direct result of this ruling, an eleven-year-old Aboriginal girl with leukemia was pulled from chemotherapy and taken to a holistic healing centre in Florida. The judge refused to order the Children's Aid Society to take over guardianship of the child and readmit her into chemotherapy, which had a 90 to 95 percent chance of success. Without the therapy, she was almost certain to die.[120]

It is apparent that human rights have become the common vernacular for framing grievances. Consider, for instance, the Canadian Museum for Human Rights' massive nationwide consultation in 2009. The consultations visited 17 cities, convened 357 group meetings, and spoke to 1,222 individuals. The committee met with educators, activists, artists, lawyers, and a range of other professionals from various religious, ethnic, racial, and class backgrounds. It was the most comprehensive dialogue on human rights in Canadian history. More than anything else, the committee's consultations demonstrated just how extensive rights inflation has become in Canada. In discussing the plight of Aboriginal peoples, individuals framed a wide range of problems as human rights violations: loss of language, culture, and belief systems; the breaking up of families; distrust of police; assault on children; the adoption by European Canadians of First Nations children; missing and murdered Aboriginal women; and the large number of children in foster homes. Poverty and violence against women were repeatedly raised as issues: several participants described these as the most widespread (and tolerated) human rights abuses in the world. Discussions around children's rights led to debate about bullying. Some argued that the failure to provide learning support for children with a disability violated children's rights and condemned them to a life of underemployment and social exclusion. Prisoners' rights advocates spoke about incarceration and the absence of legal aid as human rights violations. Many of the participants in the hearings also emphasized economic, social, and environmental justice. Nova Scotia's Human Rights Commission suggested that poverty, which is a social condition, was a systemic human rights violation.[121]

Social media provide another example of how common it is for Canadians to articulate their grievances in terms of human rights. For instance, in 2018 there were at least fifty-three Facebook pages dedicated to human rights in Canada. Most of these sites were being managed by human rights commissions, civil liberties or human rights associations, universities, or the Canadian Museum for Human Rights. There are also Facebook pages devoted to lobbying for the inclusion of gender identity in human rights legislation and to promoting the Toronto Gay Pride Parade. Twitter is emerging as another vehicle for advancing human rights claims. In addition to all this, a host of Twitter accounts frame HIV, LGBT youth, drug policy, climate change, and collective bargaining as human rights issues.[122]

Canadians have also taken enthusiastically to blogging about human rights. The blogosphere is one of the most popular media for conversing about human rights. As of 2018 there were well over a hundred blogs dedicated to human rights in Canada. All of them reflected the issues of the day. Predictably, some of these blogs spew right-wing hate-mongering that does little to enrich the conversation. Most of them are critical of human rights law, especially prohibitions on hate speech or discrimination against homosexuals.[123] Many human rights blogs, however, discuss education, privacy, the needs of the elderly, second-hand smoking in condominiums, smart meters, and equality rights for the disabled. Several blogs routinely comment on decisions handed down by human rights commissions. Others are devoted to Indigenous women; mental illness; foreign policy; sex workers' health and safety; hate speech; autistic children; same-sex marriage; assisted suicide; age discrimination; accountability for Canadian corporations operating abroad; food; the environment; and child welfare. In each case, the issue under discussion is framed as a human right.

Clearly, there exists a rich discussion among Canadians about human rights. This sort of dialogue is an essential element of any rights culture; it is through such dialogue that future rights claims are likely to emerge. But this raises questions about the widespread use of rights talk. These days, almost every grievance is framed as a human right. For example, in response to the housing crisis on the Aboriginal reserve of Attawapiskat, many commentators framed housing, health, and education as human rights.[124] The McGill Human Rights Interns' blog lists a host of rights claims, including ones related to supplemental health care benefits for refugees, access to HIV services, and the lack of drug and alcohol treatment centres in Iqaluit.[125] A few blogs focused on labour law have drawn attention to human rights violations in the workplace, notably termination without cause, inadequate health and safety, and privacy violations (the monitoring of Internet use, the accessing of content on workplace computers, the requirement to provide social media passwords).[126] The John Humphrey Centre for Peace and Human Rights uses its blog and its Facebook and Twitter accounts to promote human rights as "needs that everyone is entitled to for a quality of life and well-being."[127]

Social movements are another important incubator for emerging rights claims. Egale Canada insists that young people should be free of harassment, regardless of sexual orientation, and suggests that there is a human right to "a safe learning environment, free from harassment."[128] The rights of transgendered people are part of a new generation of rights claims. Egale supports amendments to human rights legislation so as to include "gender identity" and "gender expression" as protected grounds of discrimination.[129] Aboriginal peoples too are framing their grievances in the language of rights. The BC Métis Federation brought complaints under federal and provincial human rights legislation arguing that the decision to fund only its rival organization (the Métis National Council) was discriminatory.[130] Another leading Aboriginal rights organization, the Assembly of First Nations (AFN), has gone to great efforts to integrate the United Nations' *Declaration of the Rights of Indigenous Peoples* into its advocacy.[131] The AFN believes that Indigenous rights in Canada should be modelled on that Declaration. Those rights are divided into three broad categories: the right to self-determination; culture, language, and education rights; and land rights and the environment. Another prominent issue is the right to clean water. The AFN, drawing on the language of the Declaration, is lobbying to have access to clean water recognized as a human right.[132] There is growing support to recognize Aboriginal peoples' environmental rights, mineral rights, and access to clean water and affordable housing as human rights.[133] The Union of BC Indian Chiefs believes that the non-development of ancestral lands that include burial grounds is Aboriginal peoples' human right.[134] The Native Aboriginal Women's Association has declared that violence against women is Canada's number-one human rights issue.[135]

Anti-poverty organizations such as the Ontario Coalition Against Poverty (OCAP) are similarly engaged in rights talk. OCAP lobbied for the release of activists jailed for participating in a roadblock in support of Secwepemc territorial and cultural rights, specifically in relation to the 2001 demolition of homes on Secwepemc territories by Sun Peaks Resort.[136] The organization is also concerned about the rights of the poor with disabilities. A recent case involved a person with cerebral palsy who relied on a facilitator to communicate and was denied service at a Toronto restaurant.[137] OCAP has raised further concerns regarding the rights of refugees, immigrants, and migrant workers. They have framed a recent attempt to deport a Filipino live-in caregiver as a human rights violation. According to OCAP, live-in caregivers are often not informed of their rights when they arrive in Canada, and the federal government has failed to uphold their mobility and family rights. In the case of Eleanora Carag, she faced the prospect of being permanently separated from her Canadian-born child if deported.[138] OCAP is not the only anti-poverty organization that frames grievances as human rights. The BC Poverty Reduction Coalition is even more direct: "The existence of poverty in British Columbia is a violation of human rights."[139]

Social movements are pushing at the boundaries of our rights culture. According to the West Coast Legal Education and Action

Fund, the lack of available child care violates the human rights of women and children.[140] The Elizabeth Fry Society insists that the use of punitive force against female prisoners is a violation of human rights. The organization has filed a complaint with the United Nations on behalf of all women in Canadian federal prisons who are Aboriginal or have mental health issues.[141] The Council of Canadians with Disabilities, which describes itself as a national human rights organization, frames most of its advocacy in terms of human rights, whether it relates to housing, assisted suicide, or accessibility and services for people with disabilities.[142] According to the Canadian Association of the Deaf, communication is a human right, as is using sign language and having access to VOIP services.[143] The Canadian Council of Muslim Women views banning the niqab and hijab as necessary in order to ensure women's rights.[144] The United Church supports water as a human right; it also advocates for education, universal health care, sustainable healthy communities, and security for Indigenous women as human rights.[145] The National Association of Women and the Law has identified a host of grievances as human rights violations: poverty, restrictions on access to abortion, national security policies that target immigrant women, inhumane prisons, and punitive immigration and refugee policies.[146] PIVOT, Greenpeace, B'nai Brith, the Canadian Labour Congress, and the Canadian Conference of Catholic Bishops have similarly identified a host of issues as rights concerns: homelessness, housing, access to medical treatment, police misconduct, exploitation of sex workers, access to clean water, self-determination, peace, pay equity, security, child care, collective bargaining, labour mobility, and human trafficking, among others. Women Against Violence Against Women and the YWCA frame gender-based violence and the sexual exploitation of women as human rights violations.[147] Vancouver Rape Relief (VRR) believes that a man's ability to pay for sexual access to other humans often supersedes a woman's right to not be involved in prostitution.[148] From this perspective, prostitution is a violation of human rights, and women are uniquely vulnerable to this rights violation.

There is nothing new about many of these grievances. Women, after all, have been advocating for pay equity and day care for generations, and Aboriginal peoples have demanded land and resources for just as long. What is historically recent is that they are now framing these grievances as human rights.[149] Human rights have become the dominant idiom for challenging anything that is unfair. Without a doubt, these are all legitimate grievances. We should not ignore how vulnerable groups in our community are being marginalized by poverty or addiction. But are these grievances best framed as human rights?

We are entering a historically unique moment in Canada when human rights will be used to frame virtually any grievance. The problem has to do with the conflation of human rights with social justice.[150] During the 2014 Quebec election's leaders' debate, Françoise David, the leader of Québec solidaire, insisted that health care was "un droit fondamentale et une question de justice sociale." But we must distinguish between social justice and human rights. That distinction is not meant to prioritize human rights over social justice; rather, it is about how best to pursue social justice while protecting human rights. Social justice is the pursuit of equality.[151] It refers to those conditions that enable individuals to seek out their conception of the good life.[152] We should reject the impulse to frame all grievances as human rights. As James Griffin points out, "human rights have been proliferating at such a suspect rate because we all want to cash in on the power of the language of rights. But why not instead recover and protect the power of justice? It is a great mistake to think that, because we see rights as especially important in morality, we must make everything especially important in morality into a right."[153]

Social justice is, as Amartya Sen suggests, the "capability to lead the kind of lives we have reason to value."[154] It combines a commitment to economic and social equality with the fair distribution of resources. It is how society's institutions determine the division of advantages and resources derived from social cooperation.[155] It requires removing obstacles to freedom such as poverty and lack of economic opportunity. Human rights have a role to play in realizing social justice: they are essential for recognizing injustice and facilitating the emergence of new social values. Human rights are, as Sen argues, essential to social and economic development.[156]

Issues like poverty are best framed as social justice rather than human rights. The distinction is an important one. As Sen argues,

> the emergence of a shared recognition of that "injustice" may be dependent in practice on open discussion of issues and feasibilities ... The role of public discussion to debate conventional wisdom on both practicalities and valuations can be central to the acknowledgement of injustice ... Basic civil rights and political freedoms are indispensible for the emergence of social values. Indeed, the freedom to participate in critical evaluation and in the process of value formation is among the most crucial freedoms of societal existence.[157]

Another way of conceiving of social justice is in terms of political participation, respect for cultural diversity, and access to protections and benefits.[158] Social change is inherent in the very notion of social justice, which provides the natural language for moral claims that distinguish right from wrong. Demands for social justice are almost always a product of grassroots movements organized by those seeking empowerment and social inclusion.[159] Human rights, for their part, *facilitate* social justice. There is, to be sure, a relationship between human rights and social justice, but the two should not be conflated. "Social justice," Brian Barry tells us, "should be conceived of as building on the foundation of liberal rights."[160] Rights are essential for recognizing injustice and facilitating the emergence of new social values.

Two recent cases highlight the tendency to conflate human rights with social justice. Jeffrey Moore, who was diagnosed with a severe learning disability (dyslexia) in elementary school, was receiving remedial teaching until funding cuts led to the elimination of the facility he attended. His parents placed him in private school. But they successfully argued before the BC Human Rights

Tribunal that by failing to provide this service, the school board was discriminating against Moore on the basis of his disability. In 2012 the Supreme Court of Canada reaffirmed the tribunal's decision and ordered the school board to provide adequate services to students with learning disabilities.[161] No fewer than seven of Canada's human rights commissions intervened in court to support this interpretation of the law. Meanwhile, the First Nations Child and Family Caring Society of Canada had filed a complaint in 2007 with the Canadian Human Rights Commission. They claimed that the federal government was underfunding child welfare services compared to provincial programs. It was their assertion that this practice constituted discrimination on the basis of race and national or ethnic origin in the provision of services. In 2016 the Canadian Human Rights Tribunal ruled—after the Federal Court ordered the tribunal to hear a case it originally rejected as beyond its mandate—that underfunding on reserves was discrimination and therefore a violation of the *Canadian Human Rights Act*.[162]

Both cases exemplify how rights talk, along with human rights law, is being appropriated to create social programs that address a range of grievances.[163] These types of cases have the potential to turn human rights commissions into forums for determining the legitimacy of cuts to social programs by framing funding for social services as a human right. Such cases frame not just access to social services as a human right, but also the creation and distribution of social services.

A common justification for rights inflation is that Canada is simply fulfilling its international obligations.[164] Several international treaties, for instance, recognize a right to education and health care. But this argument is unconvincing. True, Canada has acceded to numerous treaties. None of those treaties, however, have been incorporated wholesale into Canadian law. Human rights treaties are aspirational. Judges may occasionally cite international treaties, but treaties do not determine the law.[165] Human rights treaties depend on states to interpret and implement law. The principles espoused in international treaties are purposefully written as abstract values.[166] *The Convention on Economic, Social and*

Cultural Rights includes the right to food, for instance, but it does not specify how much food or who is responsible (and how) for distribution. Rather, principles espoused under international law are to be applied by governments in ways that are consistent with their own rights cultures. To suggest that treaties require the recognition of new rights in Canada ignores the reality of international law and the role of states in enforcing human rights. Besides, there is something disconcerting about suggesting that domestic policy should be determined by institutions we did not elect as a consequence of treaties that we cannot amend on our own.[167]

Framing grievances in the language of rights is neither automatic nor inevitable—it is a choice. There are many reasons why rights inflation remains the defining social and political trend of our time.[168] As Griffin notes:

> The belief is widespread that human rights mark what is most important in morality; so whatever any group in society regards as most important, it will be strongly tempted to declare to be a human right ... It is now also a common, and not unjustified, belief that getting something widely accepted as a human right is a good first step to getting it made a legal right ... And getting something accepted as a human right transforms one's case. One is transformed from beggar ("you ought to help me") to chooser ("it is mine by right").[169]

Since the 1990s, organizations around the world that have traditionally focused on civil and political rights, including Amnesty International and Human Rights Watch, have committed resources to advocating for a much broader range of grievances. Meanwhile, there has been a perceptible shift among social justice movements.[170] Anti-poverty and humanitarian organizations, such as Oxfam and Save the Children, are making the strategic choice of framing long-standing concerns such as poverty, access to education, and AIDS prevention and treatment as human rights issues.[171] For social movements, human rights are an effective master frame for mobilizing people in support of an issue and for pressuring opponents. Human rights talk lends legitimacy to grievances and provides a common language capable of unifying a diverse constituency. Human rights laws are also an attractive option for people and groups because they provide an established institutional framework for pursuing grievances. Through local, national, and international agencies, the human rights legal system offers quasi-judicial mechanisms that are useful for activists seeking redress against their own governments. Even if legal remedies are limited, any institutional recognition of a new right can mobilize supporters and enhance the legitimacy of a claim. Environmentalists, for instance, are increasingly drawn to framing environmental degradation as a rights violation because international treaties offer no recourse to individuals who are victims of environmental harm. As one author has suggested, deforestation might be framed as a human rights violation instead of ecological devastation:

> We could indicate that the peoples displaced by the cutting are indigenous peoples that have a symbiotic and cultural connection to their land. Removing them to another area is a violation of their human rights to life ... We can focus our case on a number of rights, including the right to life, the right to an effective judicial remedy, the right to the benefit of culture, the right to be free from interference with one's home, the right of minorities, the right to identity, and others.[172]

The demand is growing for the human right to a safe and ecologically balanced environment to be recognized in law. By resorting to human rights to frame their grievances, environmentalists are contributing to rights inflation. And they have been remarkably successful. Before 1972, no country recognized a clean and healthy environment as a constitutional right. Today, 147 out of 193 United Nations member countries have constitutional protections for the environment. These provisions take the form of a government duty to protect the environment or an individual right to a healthy environment (and a duty of individuals to protect the environment). In at least fifty-six constitutions, the right to a healthy environment is classified as a fundamental human right.[173] This is an astonishing instance of the widespread recognition of a new right in a single generation.

Undoubtedly there are some minor historical precedents for many current rights claims. It might be possible to find precedents in the past of someone claiming a right to clean water or a healthy environment, although there is no history of such claims gaining popular appeal until recently. The crucial difference, however, lies in understanding the historical context. With a few famous exceptions such as the United States Bill of Rights, it is only in recent history that human rights have been codified in law. The establishment of institutional mechanisms such as human rights commissions to pursue rights claims is also a historically recent phenomenon. There were barely a dozen national human rights institutions in the world in 1980; today, most of the world's countries have one (or are now creating one).[174] This astounding proliferation of comparable institutions across regions, cultures, and legal systems is a testament to the profound impact that human rights has had on domestic law. Someone claiming a human right to water or social assistance would have been easily dismissed a generation ago. Today, such a claim has greater resonance. It builds on other precedents in human rights and can employ institutional mechanisms to gain legitimacy and recognition. This is especially the case in Canada, which has one of the most robust human rights legal systems in the world. As a result, human rights commissions and tribunals are becoming the battleground for rights inflation.

Yet human rights should not be the language we use to frame every possible injustice.[175] We should reject attempts to frame the environment or food as human rights, not because they are less important, but because human rights offers a poor language for articulating such grievances. Decisions as to when and where to take resources from others in order to provide education or health care must be negotiable, because neither is an absolute right. Human rights is a discourse of absolutes: such rights are non-negotiable principles. Framing grievances as human rights places them above the pragmatic considerations of policy-making.[176] It frames the issue in stark terms and thus limits any option for compromise. As Stefan-Ludwig Hoffman notes, human rights is "often evoked as a last-resort trumping argument in broader foundational debates.

Indeed, in advocacy situations, most human rights professionals will take human rights law as their starting point, with the latter's facticity being seen as a sort of magical fiat, a pre-ordained ground which is beyond questioning."[177]

Social justice, unlike human rights, is negotiable in that it is contingent on a society's available resources. Why recognize Jeffrey Moore's right to publicly funded tutoring and not the quality of education and health care for Aboriginal peoples on reserves? Perhaps the answer is to recognize all of these grievances as human rights. But resources are not unlimited, so it is inevitable that providing educational resources to students will require that resources be withdrawn from others. Framing the issue as a human right sets the stage for a deadlocked conflict between social actors who have come to understand their grievances as non-negotiable rights. It also provides a useful justification for governments to deny resources to those in need by insisting that they are fulfilling the human rights of others.

The existence of a human right must be premised on the ability of the state and society to guarantee such rights. This is not to say that protecting core rights is free. On the contrary, legal systems also require redistribution of resources besides facing hard choices. But it is axiomatic that the cost of enforcing core rights is a viable social practice compared to the impossible aspiration of guaranteeing remedy for all grievances that are today framed as human rights. As Aryeh Neier, the co-founder of Human Rights Watch, has insisted, "although there certainly will be economic ramifications of efforts to enforce such rights, they do not involve a broad redistribution of society's resources or its economic burdens. Therefore, I would distinguish the incidental costs of protecting civil and political rights from the much more substantial costs of economic redistribution."[178] The existence of a human right must be premised on the ability of the state and society to guarantee such rights. Rights inflation forces states to make impossible choices because of limited resources.

In other words, we must defend Jeffrey Moore's right to attend school regardless of his learning disability. At the same time, we have a shared responsibility to attempt to redistribute resources to provide the proper education to ensure that he is not disadvantaged because the curriculum makes it impossible for him to learn and share in the same opportunities as other students. This is not an argument for creating a hierarchy of rights. In fact, one reason why we must reject rights inflation is to avoid hierarchies of rights. Resources in our society are finite, and any attempt to recognize all rights claims today would force us to prioritize some rights claims above others, or recognize none at all. Rejecting the human rights frame for these issues in no way denies the ethical or moral legitimacy of such grievances.

Furthermore, framing a grievance as a human right almost inevitably makes it a legal issue, whereas framing an issue as a question of social justice implies a broader societal problem that requires systemic solutions.[179] The distinction between legal rights and human rights, as Costas Douzinas argues, is becoming increasingly blurred.[180] In Lisa Vanhala's study of activism among people with disabilities in Canada, she found a direct link between framing grievances as human rights and the movement's focus on litigation as a strategy for social change.[181] Yet as Richard Wilson notes, the "legalization of rights is mystifying (in the historical materialist sense) insofar as it raises false expectations that the state can solve social and economic problems, and normalizing, insofar as it employs the legal/bureaucratic system but does not challenge it."[182] There is a well-developed scholarship that attacks North American rights cultures as excessively legalistic and individualistic.[183] Judges, according to some critics, are prone to ignore the broader needs of the community in favour of the narrow desires of individuals. Many of these same critics insist that rights foster a sense of entitlement rather than duties or responsibilities to the community. This is not an argument about the policy-making powers of the judiciary. Framing issues of social justice as human rights violations is counterproductive because a rights approach fails to address the root causes of these social problems.

Many social problems require far more systemic solutions than the legal system can provide.[184] Human rights scholars are increasingly raising concerns about rights-based activism. As Dorothy Hodgson argues,

> a growing number of scholars, policy-makers, and activists have become increasingly wary of the dominance of rights-based approaches to social justice and, increasingly, development ... The demand of women (and men) in the global south for economic justice in the face of repeated efforts by states, elites and capital to alienate their land and undermine their livelihoods in the name of particular neoliberal visions of "progress" and "productivity" reveals the limits of legal frameworks for obtaining social justice. Part of the problem is that rights-based protocols empower states—the very entities most often accused of violating the rights of individuals and collectivities—with the power to implement and enforce laws to protect their rights. But nation-states are far more likely to selectively enforce the rights of privileged individuals than to guarantee collective rights for groups, whether indigenous, minority or women.[185]

The close association of rights with law encourages people and movements to pursue limited legal solutions to complex social problems.[186] For instance, a rights-based approach to resisting cuts to social programs for children with autism has exacerbated tensions within the movement of people with disabilities. Legal strategies often depend on a medicalized model of disability, which conflicts with activism premised on disability as a social construction.[187] Similarly, many transnational feminist advocates insist that rights-based activism is effective for fact-finding projects, but ineffective for addressing systemic oppression in patriarchal societies.[188] Hodgson draws a similar conclusion in the context of gender-based violence:

> We need to be alert to the ways in which discourses about gender-based violence and the suffering of women create particular cultural and political subjects, which often accompany and can come to subvert some of the other powerful enabling ideas of human rights. Human Rights positions itself as a neutral field of equality for all. Such a claim of neutrality, however, denies the myriad ways in which ideas about what it means to be a

woman, about the proper relations between men and women, about the existence of a private and a public sphere, for example, structure the demands and expectations of rights.[189]

Framing issues such as violence against women as rights violations requires women to articulate their grievances in a gender-neutral language rather as than discourses about power. In the legal battles surrounding the rape shield law in Canada, for example, feminist organizations such as the Legal Education Action Fund were forced to frame their arguments in terms of equality rights rather than how to best address women's sexual subordination, which was the root of their argument in campaigning for the law.[190] As a result, the social construction of sexuality and the relations of power that produce sexual inequality are neglected or ignored with rights-based activism.[191] Men have taken advantage of this opportunity to exploit the equality provisions in the constitution. Organizations such as the National Association of Women and the Law have been forced to spend time and resources defending legislative reforms that they had spent years to secure. Meanwhile, the men's rights movement has won several notable legal victories that have placed women on the defensive on issues such as child custody, naming children, and sexual assault.[192] These cases highlight the failure to address the specific historical and social relations of power facing women when they are forced to frame issues in the language of rights.

The rights inflation of recent years is most problematic when we try to turn principles of social justice into justiciable legal rights. With a few notable examples, in no country have the courts been capable of redistributing resources to alleviate disparities in wealth. Attempts to do so in places like India and South Africa, whose constitutions recognize economic and social rights, have proven futile.[193] Litigation in Brazil to enforce a right to health care has resulted in demands for expensive medicines, which the government has refused to provide because of a lack of funds.[194] It is also worth noting that despite trends among social justice movements worldwide, there remains some opposition to framing grievances as human rights. There are still movements that prefer to frame grievances such as hunger or poverty in religious terms; meanwhile, non-partisan organizations fear that a rights-based approach will undermine their neutrality. A more common concern is that human rights are an ineffective strategy because they are associated with legal remedies.[195] Rights talk leads activists to address their grievances through legal means, yet these social problems require far more systemic solutions than the legal system can provide.

There is something profoundly inadequate about rights talk when it comes to systemic social problems.[196] Perhaps denying James Moore the resources he needed at school was—as his parents argued in court—discrimination on the basis of disability. Yet constructing Moore as a person with a disability did little or nothing to address systemic problems: how curricula are produced, the lack of awareness surrounding learning disabilities, the presumption that people with disabilities are not normal and need special treatment, and the bullying and shaming Moore often faced at school. Human rights is a poor language for addressing such a complex issue.

Rights inflation has many other implications. How are human rights commissions responding to the host of new complaints? When founding a museum dedicated to human rights, are we to include every possible grievance? What should we teach as human rights in schools? How are we to distinguish between rights and non-rights when confronted with incidents that we all feel are unfair? What do we promote or assert as human rights abroad? How are we to assess the human rights performance of other nations, especially when it is a determining factor in the provision of humanitarian aid or the imposition of sanctions? In a recent study, Freedman and Mchangama showed how countries with poor human rights mandates, such as Cuba, routinely vote to expand the mandate of the UN's Special Rapporteurs. This form of "rights proliferation" benefits human rights abusers by diluting the focus of Special Rapporteurs.[197] It is far more difficult for them to determine when many of these rights—which often address systemic inequalities such as poverty or inadequate housing—have been violated. The effect has been to shift the UN's resources away from more identifiable rights violations that might lead to intervention. At the same time, in an era when human rights are an integral component of international politics, rights inflation increases the possibility of forceful intervention against other states. Even if one does not accept that the wars in Kosovo and Afghanistan, among others, were motivated by a desire to protect human rights, there is no doubt that such an appeal made the conflict more palatable to the public.[198]

Human rights enable the pursuit of social justice. They allow citizens to engage in campaigns for free public education, access to health care, insurance for the unemployed, a minimum amount of food for all citizens, access to housing for the homeless, clean water on reserves, and many other things. Canada has one of the most expansive human rights legal systems in the world, yet none of Canada's human rights laws could be fairly described as designed to ameliorate systemic inequalities.[199] Past rights claims, such as rights for sexual minorities and people with disabilities, have operated within the framework of equal treatment: the principle is that socially disadvantaged people have the right to equal participation in the social, economic, and political life of the country. Of course, lack of proper health care or education, especially for marginalized people such as those with disabilities, undermines the pretense of equality by restricting their ability to participate fully in society. But rejecting this form of inequality as a human right and framing it instead as a question of social justice in no way detracts from the need to address this social problem. As Douzinas argues, "human rights attempt to stop discrimination against women or gays, but they do not give full recognition to this unique woman or gay unless it takes full account of the long history of material and cultural deprivation that being 'different,' 'abnormal,' 'not fully human' has inflicted on its victims. This is the reason why the success of anti-discrimination legislation has been so limited despite good intentions."[200]

Distinguishing human rights from social justice is not an argument to prioritize the former over the latter; rather, it highlights the question of how best to pursue social justice while protecting human rights. The challenge is to find the threshold or conditions for determining what should be considered a human right. That something is morally wrong, or an injustice, does not mean it should be approached as a human rights violation. At the same time, we should be wary of assuming that the distinction is based on some awkward dichotomy between political/civil and economic/social/cultural rights.[201] Rather, human rights are the highest possible claim we can make in our society, but as legal rights they are an ineffective solution to systemic social problems. Human rights are not the only language for framing our grievances.[202] There are other institutions—or we can create new ones—to address the prominent social justice issues of the day. Freedom is a precondition for social justice. People do not starve in free and democratic societies.[203] It is beholden on us to resist its appropriation of human rights for any and all grievances.

Notes

1   Quoted in Timothy J. Stanley, *Contesting White Supremacy: School Segregation, Anti-Racism, and the Making of Chinese Canadians* (Vancouver: UBC Press, 2011), 41.

2   Carmela Patrias, "Socialists, Jews, and the 1947 Saskatchewan Bill of Rights," *Canadian Historical Review* 87, no. 2 (2006): 270.

3   For a detailed study of how people in the colonies conceived of rights and liberties, see Michel Ducharme, *Le concept de liberté au Canada à l'époque des révolutions atlantiques 1776–1838* (Montreal and Kingston: McGill–Queen's University Press, 2010); E.A. Heaman, "Rights Talk and the Liberal Order Framework," in *Liberalism and Hegemony: Debating the Canadian Revolution*, ed. Jean-François Constant and Michel Ducharme (Toronto: University of Toronto Press, 2009).

4   Janet Ajzenstat, *The Canadian Founding: John Locke and Parliament* (Montreal and Kingston: McGill–Queen's University Press, 2007).

5   These findings are based on a detailed survey of the digital archive for both newspapers. The survey included a keyword search of the terms civil liberty, civil liberties, and human right for the years 1844 to 1970, 1892 to 1897, 1910 to 1915, 1937 to 1939, and 1976 to 1977. The survey identified the title and subject for each article containing these terms.

6   Canada, *Special Joint Committee of the Senate and the House of Commons on Human Rights and Fundamental Freedoms* (Ottawa: King's Printer, 1947); *Special Committee on Human Rights and Fundamental Freedoms* (Ottawa: Queen's Printer, 1950).

7   An exception to this narrow conception was the Trades and Labour Congress, which argued for the inclusion of the right to employment and other economic rights in the constitution. Dominique Clément, *Human Rights in Canada* (Waterloo: WLU Press, 2014).

8   One of the reasons for this discursive shift was the emergence of the Co-operative Commonwealth Federation, which transformed politics in Canada. The CCF was a social democratic movement that became an influential party in federal and provincial politics beginning in the 1930s. It was not uncommon for the party to frame its grievances in the language of human rights, and to argue that property rights violated human rights.

9   For a discussion of Canada's human rights legal system and how it compares with others, see Dominique Clément, *Equality Deferred: Sex Discrimination and British Columbia's Human Rights State, 1953–1984* (Vancouver: UBC Press and the Osgoode Society for Canadian Legal History, 2014), Chapter 3; Pearl Eliadis, *Speaking Out on Human Rights: Debating Canada's Human Rights System* (Montreal and Kingston: McGill–Queen's University Press, 2014), 29–33.

10   Historian Samuel Moyn contends that human rights did not come to the fore of international politics until the 1970s because other utopian ideals, such as communism, had by then become discredited: "It was, instead, only in the 1970s that a genuine social movement around human rights made its appearance, seizing the foreground by transcending official government institutions, especially international ones." Samuel Moyn, *The Last Utopia: Human Rights in History* (Boston: Belknap Press of Harvard University Press, 2010), 8.

11   Ibid.

12   Dominique Clément, "Human Rights in Canadian Domestic and Foreign Politics: From 'Nigardly Acceptance' to Enthusiastic Embrace," *Human Rights Quarterly* 34, no. 3 (2012); Asa Mckercher, "Sound and Fury: Diefenbaker, Human Rights, and Canadian Foreign Policy," *Canadian Historical Review* 97, no. 2 (2016).

13   For a complete history of human rights in Canada, see Clément, *Human Rights in Canada*.

14   Lisa Vanhala, *Making Rights a Reality?: Disability Rights Activists and Legal Mobilization* (Cambridge: Cambridge University Press, 2010), 48–50.

15   Ibid., 54–55.

16   On rights associations, see Dominique Clément, *Canada's Rights Revolution: Social Movements and Social Change, 1937–1982* (Vancouver: UBC Press, 2008). On the women's movement, see Dominique Clément, "'I Believe in Human Rights, Not Women's Rights': Women and the Human Rights State, 1969–1984," *Radical History Review* 101 (2008). Tom Warner, *Never Going Back: A History of Queer Activism in Canada* (Toronto: University of Toronto Press, 2002).

17   Moyn, *The Last Utopia*, 12.

18   Hutterites are an Anabaptist Christian sect whose members reject personal ownership and communally own land. They are strict pacifists and refuse to vote or hold public office. Doukhobors are also a Christian pacifist sect. They live communally and have, similar to Hutterites and Jehovah's Witnesses, opposed conscription and wartime policies. Jehovah's Witnesses are pacifists who live a strict reading of the Bible and reject any displays of patriotism. They are virulently anti-Catholic and consider the Roman Catholic Church to be Satan's institution on earth. For further details

about state repression and discrimination against Hutterites, Doukhobors, and Jehovah's Witnesses, see Dominique Clément, "Alberta's Rights Revolution," *British Journal of Canadian Studies* 26, no. 1 (2013); Clément, *Canada's Rights Revolution*; William Kaplan, *Canadian Maverick: The Life and Times of Ivan C. Rand* (Toronto: University of Toronto Press, 2009), Chapter 4; Ross Lambertson, *Repression and Resistance: Canadian Human Rights Activists, 1930–1960* (Toronto: University of Toronto Press, 2005), Chapter 1.

19   Quoted in Peter N. Moogk, "The Crime of Lèse-Majesté in New France: Defence of the Secular and Religious Order," in *Canadian State Trials: Law, Politics, and Security Measures, 1608–1837*, ed. F. Murray Greenwood and Barry Wright (Toronto: University of Toronto Press, 1996), 238. The grand jury refused to indict Bédard and the other editorialists.

20   Canada, *Freedom and Security under the Law (Report of the Commission on Inquiry Concerning Certain Activities of the Royal Canadian Mounted Police)* (Ottawa: Queen's Printer, 1981).

21   For an overview of religion and human rights in Canada, including the cases noted in this section, see Mary Anne Waldron, *Free to Believe: Rethinking Freedom of Conscience and Religion in Canada* (Toronto: University of Toronto Press, 2013).

22   Jake Edmiston, "Ontario man suing county for $5000 in damages over Lord's Prayer at meetings," *National Post*, 31 July 2012.

23   No author, "In the great Toronto haircut debate, common sense should prevail" *Toronto Star*, 15 November 2012.

24   The BCCT argued that the pledge of conduct discriminated against sexual minorities. The court, however, determined that there was no evidence that graduates of TWU discriminated against homosexual students in the classroom. Waldron, *Free to Believe*, 107–9. In 2013, TWU was granted a licence to operate a law school in British Columbia. However, the law societies of Ontario and Nova Scotia have voted against recognizing law degrees from TWU.

25   Ian Mulgrew, "Province Rethinking TWY law school," *Vancouver Sun*, 19 November 2014. In 2016, however, the Nova Scotia Court of Appeal upheld a ruling that overturned the law society's ban. Ontario's Court of Appeal, however, upheld the Law Society of Upper Canada's refusal of accreditation for graduates of the university. *The Nova Scotia Barristers' Society v Trinity Western University and Brayden Volkenant* 2015 NSSC 25; *Trinity Western University v. The Law Society of Upper Canada*, 2016 ONCA 518.

26   *Trinity Western University v Law Society of Upper Canada* [2018] SCC 33.

27   Waldron, *Free to Believe*, 180–91.

28   France's Charter of Secularism at School is posted in every classroom. It prohibits students from objecting to lessons for religious reasons or from wearing religious symbols. It also requires teachers to be neutral on religious issues. These restrictions are justified on the basis of guaranteeing freedom of conscience. Paul Waldie, "How the French Promotion of Secularism Offers a Cautionary Lesson for Quebec," 20 September 2013. In a

controversial column published in the *National Post* titled "In Your Face," Christopher Hitchens argued that burqas violate the rights of citizens to be equal before the law and that we have a right to see each other's faces (he compared burqas with Ku Klux Klan hoods). Christopher Hitchens, "In Your Face," *National Post*, 12 May 2010.

29   Associated Press. "France's burkini ban overturned by the highest court," *CBC News*, 26 August 2016.

30   Lysiane Gagnon, "A veiled witnesses obstructs justice," *Globe and Mail*, 9 January 2013.

31   For examples of how Canadian courts have allowed equality rights to trump religious minority rights, see Waldron, *Free to Believe*.

32   The conflict over freedom of religion is especially divisive in Quebec. In 2010 the Liberal government introduced, but never passed, legislation to force women to uncover their faces when using public services. The government also established a Consultation Commission on Accommodation Practices Related to Cultural Differences. The commission's mandate was to investigate a spate of controversial incidents surrounding the accommodation of religious minorities. These incidents included a Muslim woman's demand for a female driving examiner, the Outremont YMCA's decision to frost its windows at the request of local Hasidic Jews, and the town of Hérouxville's code of conduct that included a ban on stoning women. Most of the commission's recommendations, however, were ignored. And it was only the Liberal Party's unexpected victory in 2014 that prevented the Charter of Quebec Values from becoming law. In 2015 the newly elected Liberal government introduced a more limited statute that would, among other things, require all public services to be received and delivered with an uncovered face (which amounted to a ban on burkas and niqabs).

33   Janice Gross Stein, ed. *Uneasy Partners: Multiculturalism and Rights in Canada* (Waterloo: Wilfrid Laurier University Press, 2007); Susan Moller Okin, "Is Multiculturalism Bad for Women?," in *Is Multiculturalism Bad for Women?*, ed. Susan Moller Okin (Princeton: Princeton University Press, 1999).

34   Another example of a fundamental freedom that remains contested is freedom of association. Police have used extraordinary measures to curb protests in Canada, most infamously during the 1997 APEC summit in Vancouver and the 2010 G20 meeting in Toronto. There is a growing tendency in recent years to criminalize the right to protest.

35   "Signora Fallaci then moves on to the livelier examples of contemporary Islam—for example, Ayatollah Khomeini's 'Blue Book' and its helpful advice on romantic matters: 'If a man marries a minor who has reached the age of nine and if during the defloration he immediately breaks the hymen, he cannot enjoy her any longer.' I'll say. I know it always ruins my evening. Also: 'A man who has had sexual relations with an animal, such as a sheep, may not eat its meat. He would commit sin.' Indeed. A quiet cigarette afterwards as you listen to your favourite Johnny Mathis LP and then a promise to call her next week and swing by the pasture is by far the best way. It may also be a sin to roast your nine-year-old wife, but the Ayatollah's not clear on that." Mark Steyn, "Celebrate Tolerance, or you're dead," *Maclean's*, 28 April 2006.

36   There were also cases in New Brunswick and Ontario involving teachers who were fired for propagating anti-Semitism. However, in these cases, they did not propagate their beliefs in school. No author, "The teachers' sideline," *Globe and Mail*, 31 August 1991; No author, "Reading, 'riting, and repression," *Globe and Mail*, 23 June 1993.

37   Whereas past complaints usually targeted white supremacist websites, the commission is now receiving complaints against people who link Muslims to violence or, because of their religious beliefs, are publicly attacking homosexuals. Richard Moon, "The Attack on Human Rights Commissions and the Corruption of Public Discourse," *Saskatchewan Law Review* 73, no. 1 (2010).

38   Pearl Eliadis, "The Controversy Entrepreneurs," *Maisonneuve* 29 (2010).

39   These data were collected from the online archives of these newspapers as well as Postmedia News with the assistance of Timothy Yu as part of a research project in 2013. See, for instance, Margaret Wente, "Free speech has to be for everyone," *Globe and Mail*, 12 February 2008; No author, "Freedom of speech," *Calgary Herald*, 14 October 2010; Andrew Coyne, "Why does Canada still have a hate speech law?," *Canada.com*, 9 July 2012; No author, "Free Speech Must Prevail," *Toronto Star*, 13 October 2012; No author, "Canada's Parliament is right to repeal Section 12 of the human rights act," *Toronto Star*, 10 June 2012; No author, "We have a right to free speech," *Ottawa Citizen*, 13 October 2012.

40   Clément, *Human Rights in Canada*.

41   There was only one attempt to establish an investigative hearing—and there no preventative arrests—before these provisions became subject to a sunset clause and were not renewed in 2007. However, the federal government amended the legislation in 2013 in the wake of the Boston bombings and reintroduced preventative detention and investigative hearings. In addition to this provision, the Act defines, for the first time in Canadian history, the crime of terrorism; however, this over-broad definition raises the danger that ordinary criminal actions will be labelled as terrorism. The rules of evidence for investigative hearings restrict the ability of defendants to challenge their detention. The Attorney General can overrule a federal judge and prohibit the disclosure (including to the defendant) of information relating to any detention. The Act also amended the hate speech section of the *Criminal Code* to facilitate removing content from the Internet.

42   In 2006 the federal government listed the Tamil Tigers as a terrorist organization and prosecuted one man for providing $3,000 to the Tamil Tigers during the civil war in Sri Lanka. He was convicted and sentenced to six months in jail. It was the first case in Canada involving terrorism financing. Among the new offences created under the *Anti-Terrorism Act* was knowingly facilitating a terrorist action, which carried a penalty of up to fourteen years in jail. "After its anti-terrorism bill was first introduced, the Canadian government was forced to add an interpretative clause stating that 'for greater certainty, the expression of a political, religious or ideological thought, belief or opinion does not come within' the definition of terrorist activity 'unless it constitutes an act or omission that satisfies the criteria of that paragraph'. The Canadian interpretative clause was

unique and demonstrates some sensitivity to claims that the legislation would contribute to discriminatory profiling." Kent Roach, "A Comparison of Australian and Canadian Anti-Terrorism Laws," *University of New South Wales Law Journal* 30, no. 1 (2007): 59. For a detailed discussion of anti-terrorism legislation, see Kent Roach, "Counter-Terrorism in and outside Canada and in and outside the Anti-Terrorism Act," *Review of Constitutional Studies / Revue d'études constitutionnelles* 16, no. 2 (2012).

43 *An Act to enact the Security of Canada Information Sharing Act and the Secure Air Travel Act, to amend the Criminal Code, the Canadian Security Intelligence Service Act and the Immigration and Refugee Protection Act and to make related and consequential amendments to other Acts,* Statutes of Canada, 2015.

44 Security certificates, which are based in immigration law and predate 9/11 (and have to be approved by a judge of the Federal Court), were meant to detain non-citizens until they could be deported. But the Supreme Court of Canada ruled that the federal government could not deport individuals if they might be tortured when they are returned to their nation of origin. The result was indefinite detention. However, some of the restrictions on due process have been successfully challenged in court, which has "led to special advocates being able to challenge the secret information and increased retention of raw intelligence that may have evidential value." Roach, "Counter-Terrorism in and outside Canada and in and outside the Anti-Terrorism Act," 256.

45 Since 9/11 more funding has been allocated towards security and intelligence gathering, and the federal government has implemented numerous programs to satisfy American security concerns. One of the key programs is the Safe Borders agreement: "These initiatives involve a series of ongoing negotiations with the United States on such matters as pre-clearance of container traffic at the point of origin; fast-tracking of safe persons and goods; collection and retention of a wide range of data on persons traveling by air across the border; the application of high-tech surveillance equipment along the border; expansion of Integrated Border Enforcement Teams; and, controversially, a "safe third country" agreement to reduce the flow of refugees across the border." Reg Whitaker, "Keeping up with the Neighbours? Canadian Responses to 9/11 in Historical and Comparative Context," *Osgoode Hall Law Journal* 41, nos. 2–3 (2003): 256.

46 Lorraine E. Weinrib, "Terrorism's Challenge to the Constitutional Order," in *The Security of Freedom: Essays on Canada's Anti-Terrorism Bill,* ed. Ronald J. Daniels, Patrick Macklem, and Kent Roach (Toronto: University of Toronto Press, 2001); Elliot Tenofsky, "The War Measures and Emergencies Acts: Implications for Canadian Civil Rights and Liberties," *American Review of Canadian Studies* 19, no. 3 (1989).

47 As Kent Roach explains, Canada "is more restrained by human rights concerns than British or Australian law ... The restraints in the [*Anti-Terrorism Act*] are praiseworthy in their commitment to legality and human rights." Roach, "Counter-Terrorism in and outside Canada and in and outside the Anti-Terrorism Act," 244, 54.

48 *Charkaoui v. Canada (Citizenship and Immigration)* [2007] 1 SCR 350.

49 GPC Research/CORA, *Listening to Canadians* (Fall 2003). Poll retrieved 10 November 2011 from the Canadian Opinion Research Archive, Queen's University.

50 Compass / National Post / Global Television, *Same-Sex: Public Embraces Gay Rights, Opposes Gay Marriage, Advocates National Referendum* (2005). Poll retrieved 6 November 2011 from http://www.compass.ca.

51 Environics Research/CORA, *Environics Focus Canada* (2010). Poll retrieved 10 November 2011 from the Canadian Opinion Research Archive, Queen's University. See also Citizen Society Research Lab / Lethbridge College, *Albertans' Opinion Structure on Six Policy Issues* (2011). Poll retrieved 10 November 2011 from http://www.lethbridgecollege.ca/about-us/applied-research-innovation/citizen-society-research-lab.

52 Ibid. Angus Reid Public Opinion. *Most Canadians Unaware of Lack of Restrictions on Abortions* (2010). Poll retrieved 12 November 2011 from http://www.visioncritical.com/category/global-opinions-and-trends.

53 One of the issues was parental leave: 81 percent of women and 77 percent of men indicated that they would support policies requiring both mothers and fathers to take parental leave. Angus Reid Public Opinion, *Gender Equality Still Elusive in Four Developed Nations* (2010). Poll retrieved 12 November 2011 from http://www.visioncritical.com/wp-content/uploads/2010/04/2010.04.19_Gender.pdf.

54 Environics Research/CORA, *Environics Focus Canada 2000* (2000). Poll retrieved 10 November 2011 from the Canadian Opinion Research Archive, Queen's University.

55 Ipsos-Reid, *Three Quarters (74%) Believe Canadian Society Less Tolerant of Others Since 9/11 Terrorist Attacks* (2011). Poll retrieved 10 November 2011 from http://www.ipsos-na.com/news-polls.

56 Ibid. An Angus Reid Strategies poll conducted in 2009 asked respondents about whether or not they held a favourable opinion towards other religions. While 72 percent had a favourable opinion towards Christianity, only 28 percent shared the same feelings about Islam. Sikhism, Hinduism, Buddhism, and Judaism were viewed favourably by less than two-thirds of those surveyed. John Geddes, "What Canadians Think of Sikhs, Jews, Christians, Muslims," *Maclean's*, 28 April 2009.

57 Eric A. Posner, *The Twilight of Human Rights Law* (New York: Oxford University Press, 2014).

58 The malleable nature of human rights has even enabled some regimes to justify repressive policies. China cites a right to development as a justification for prioritizing economic growth over political freedoms. The right to security is routinely used to frame any number of restrictions on civil liberties in countries such as Russia and Venezuela. Islamic nations appeal to the right to religious freedom to justify restrictions on women's equality.

59 Bonny Ibhawoh, "Between Culture and Constitution: Evaluating the Cultural Legitimacy of Human Rights in the African State," *Human Rights Quarterly* 22, no. 3 (2000). United Nations, General Assembly, *Declaration on the Right to Development*, 4 December 1986.

60 Friedman, *The Human Rights Culture*, 112.

61 Pete Fussey et al., *Securing and Sustaining the Olympic City: Reconfiguring London for 2012 and Beyond* (Farnham: Ashgate, 2011), 36.

62 Canada has not entrenched freedom of information in the constitution. However, Robert J. Hayward has framed the issue as an emerging right in Canada: "The concern of researcher access to government records as outlined in the Access Directive was but one limited facet of the trend during the late 1960s and early 1970s towards 'openness in government' and the concept of the public's 'right to know.' Researcher access was defined in terms of permission and the longterm, namely thirty years after the creation of the information, whereas the public policy issue known generally as freedom of information was defined in terms of the right of the citizen to full, objective, and timely information and the obligation of the State to provide such information." Robert J. Hayward, "Federal Access and Privacy Legislation and the Public Archives of Canada," *Archivaria* 18, no. 1 (1984): 49.

63 *Bronskill v Minister of Canadian Heritage* [2011] FC 983.

64 Erik Tucker, "The Constitutional Right to Bargain Collectively: The Ironies of Labour History in the Supreme Court of Canada," *Labour / Le Travail* 61, no. 1 (2008).

65 *Saskatchewan Federation of Labour v Saskatchewan* [2015] SCC 4. In a similar ruling, the Supreme Court of Canada ruled that the federal government's restrictions on RCMP members' right to organize and strike violated their freedom of association. The Court delayed the decision for a year to give the government an opportunity to revise its procedures. *Mounted Police Association of Ontario v Canada (Attorney General)* [2015] SCC 1.

66 *Canada (Attorney General) v. Bedford* [2013] SCC 72.

67 *Carter v Canada (Attorney General)* [2015] SCC 5.

68 In the past, human rights have been largely associated with the political left, which was at the forefront of campaigns for human rights law. Social democratic, liberal, and conservative governments have all written and passed human rights laws in Canada: Tommy Douglas' New Democratic Party in Saskatchewan created the first bill of rights; the Progressive Conservative government of John Diefenbaker passed the *Bill of Rights*; and the Liberal Party of Pierre Trudeau introduced the *Charter of Rights and Freedoms*. Still, it was communists, social democrats, and liberals who initiated and sustained campaigns for codifying human rights. While the right has historically been associated with defending authority, social hierarchy, and elitism, human rights have popularized principles of equality and diversity that have long been associated with the left.

69 Jan Eckel, "The Rebirth of Politics from the Spirit of Morality: Explaining the Human Rights Revolution of the 1970s," in *The Breakthrough: Human Rights in the 1970s*, ed. Jan Eckel and Samuel Moyn (Philadelphia: University of Pennsylvania Press, 2014), 248–49.

70 Nicolas *Guilhot, "International Human Rights versus Democracy Promotion*: On Two Different Meanings of Human Rights in US Foreign Policy," in *Making Human Rights Intelligible: Towards a Sociology of Human Rights*, ed. Mikael Rask Madsen and Gert Verschraegen (Portland: Hart Publishing, 2013).

71 As Tom Frarer, the former president of the Inter-American Commission on Human Rights of the Organization of American States, suggests, "whenever a phrase acquires the power to mobilize public opinion, competitors in

a democratic electoral system will struggle, within the broad limits of their respective political identities, to appropriate it. Since the mobilizing power of a phrase lies in its capacity to evoke without benefit of discussion and argument intense feelings of affection or revulsion toward some group of people or some event, institution, or transaction in the world of brute fact, then, assuming equal access of contending forces to the media of communications, with respect to any given symbol the struggle for appropriation ought to be unequal." Tom Farer, "Un-Just War against Terrorism and the Struggle to Appropriate Human Rights," *Human Rights Quarterly* 30, no. 2 (2008): 356–57.

72 *Friedmann v. MacGarvie* [2012] BCCA 445. See also "Sexual harassment counts as discrimination, BC court rules," *Globe and Mail*, 8 November 2012.

73 Wallace Immen, "How an ethnic sounding name may affect the job hunt," *Globe and Mail*, 17 November 2011; Nicholas Keung, "Ontario survey focuses on immigrants' need for Canadian experience in job market," *Toronto Star*, 5 October 2012.

74 *Eadie v. Riverbend Bed and Breakfast (No. 2)* [2012] 74 CHRR 247 (BCHRT). See also Canadian Press, "Gay couple wins human rights battle after reservation cancelled at Christian B&B," *Canada.com*, 18 July 2012.

75 Commission des droits de la personne et des droits de la jeunesse, *Systemic Discrimination Towards Migrant Workers* (Quebec: Queen's Printer, 2011).

76 Sunny Dhillon, "Could a B.C. human-rights case reveal the recipe for Timbits?," *Globe and Mail*, 27 March 2014.

77 Canadian Press, "55 African tree planters awarded $600,000 for discrimination in B.C. camp," *Globe and Mail*, 23 May 2014.

78 Canadian Press. "N.S. Human Rights Commission holds inquiry to examine restaurant washroom access," *Times Colonist*, 3 July 2018.

79 No author, "An Agency Well Pruned," *Globe and Mail*, 1 December 2006. For a more thorough review of how governments have undermined many of the women's movement's achievements in state policy, see Janine Brodie, "The Great Undoing: State Formation, Gender Politics and Social Policy in Canada," in *Western Welfare in Decline: Globalization and Women's Poverty*, ed. Catherine Kingfisher (Philadelphia: University of Pennsylvania Press, 2002).

80 Jonathan Kay, "Human rights commissions have had their day," *National Post*, 6 March 2013.

81 Women form the majority of the poor in Canada. A majority of lone-parent families headed by women are poor. Almost half of single, widowed, or divorced women are poor. The poverty rate for senior women is more than double that of men. One-third of women on their own who are over 65 years old live in poverty. Women and youth account for 83 percent of Canada's minimum-wage workers; more than one-third of lone mothers with paid employment must raise a family on an income of less than $10 per hour. Lorne Tepperman, James Curtis, and Albert Kwan, *Social Problems: A Canadian Perspective* (Toronto: Oxford University Press, 2011), 99.

82 Lipp v *Maverick's Sports Lounge*, 2014 BCHRT 199; Natalie Stechyson and Bradley Bouzane, "Pregnant women targets of 'medieval' discrimination in Canada," *National Post*, 9 March 2012; No author, "Company that dismissed pregnant B.C. employee ordered to pay \$11,000," *Georgia Straight*, 3 August 2012; Angela Hall, "Discrimination due to pregnancy flagged," *Leader Post*, 10 August 2011; No author, "Fired pregnant hair stylist awarded \$14,000," *Guelph Mercury*, 18 August 2013.

83 One *Vancouver Sun* columnist suggested that these decisions violate private property rights. Chris Schafer, "Tribunal tramples on private property rights," *Vancouver Sun*, 1 August 2012.

84 *Garrie v. Janus Joan Inc. (No. 5)* [2012] 75 CHRR 1955 (HRTO). See also Karena Walter, "Human rights victory for St. Catharines worker," *St. Catharines Standard*, 20 October 2012.

85 Peggy Curan, "An aura of mistrust still lingers," *Montreal Gazette*, 9 November 2011. Max Harrold, "Judge dismisses case, citing racial profiling," *Montreal Gazette*, 29 September 2012.

86 *O.P.T. and M.P.T. v Presteve Foods Ltd.* 2015 HRTO 675.

87 *McIntosh v. Metro Aluminum Products Ltd.* [2011] 72 CHRR 34 (BCHRT). See also No author, "\$30,000 awarded in texting case," *Vancouver Sun*, 18 February 2011.

88 *S.S. v. Taylor (No. 2)* [2012] CHRR 1839 (HRTO).

89 Technology is also raising new rights conflicts. Marlise Munoz, a thirty-three-year-old woman living Fort Worth, Texas, collapsed on her kitchen floor in November 2013 from a blood clot. Although Munoz had made it clear to her family before the accident that she would never want to be kept alive by artificial means, doctors refused to take her off life support: Munoz was fourteen weeks pregnant. Thirty-one states have laws prohibiting doctors from removing life support for pregnant patients; this has been framed as pitting the right to life against the right to die. Manny Fernandez and Erik Eckholm, "Pregnant, and Forced to Stay on Life Support," *New York Times*, 7 January 2014. Technology is also changing how we define human rights. A 2011 United Nations report, supported by France and Estonia among others, suggested that Internet connectivity is a human right. Michael Geist, "Is Internet connectivity a human right?" *Toronto Star*, 19 June 2011; Vinton Cerf, "Internet access is not a human right," *New York Times*, 3 January 2012; no author, "Web-based hate activity on the rise," *The Gazette* (Montreal), 12 April 2011.

90 Emily Bazelon, "Do Online Death Threats Count as Free Speech?," *New York Times*, 25 November 2014.

91 Patrick Brethour, "Olympic dreams of female ski jumpers take flight," *Globe and Mail*, 7 January 2008, A1; Matthew Sekeres, "Quoth the Eagle: Female jumpers not ready to soar," *Globe and Mail*, 18 January 2008, A3.

92 Jeff Gray, "Female players say fake soccer turf violates Charter, threaten legal action," *Globe and Mail*, 5 August 2014.

93 Rheal Seguin, "Quebec rights body rules against veil in health-card case," *Globe and Mail*, 19 March 2010; Rheal Seguin, "Quebec body rules against right to wear niqab," *Globe and Mail*, 17 March 2010.

94 *Olorenshaw v. Western Assurance Co.* [2013] CHRR 280 (HRTO). In another case, young renters complained that age restrictions in condominiums were discriminatory. Evan Duggan, "Gay renters face discrimination," *Vancouver Sun*, 27 August 2011; no author, "Adult-only provision shouldn't be in declaration," *Toronto Star*, 3 December 2011.

95 The award was later reduced to $6,500. The casino was involved in several other human rights cases between 2009 and 2012. *Seguin v. Great Blue Heron Charity Casino (No. 1)* [2007] 61 CHRR 3 (HRTO). See also Paul Waldie, "Gender bias in casino's washroom, court rules," *Globe and Mail*, 15 September 2008.

96 *Ismail v. British Columbia (Human Rights Tribunal) (No. 4)* [2011] 72 CHRR 101 (BCHRT). See also Terri Theodore, "Anti-lesbian rant costly for comedian and club owner," *Globe and Mail*, 21 June 2013.

97 Nicole Ireland, "Women and Dress Code Discrimination: 3 Cases That Made It to Human Rights Tribunals," *CBC News*, 5 March 2016.

98 *Gibson v. Ridgeview Restaurant Ltd. (No. 4)* [2013] CHRR 1163 (HRTO). See also John Goddard, "Marijuana or booze? Restaurant must decide," *Toronto Star*, 10 February 2009.

99 The case was later overturned by the Ontario Superior Court. *Audmax Inc. v. Ontario (Human Rights Tribunal) (No. 2)* [2009] 68 CHRR 1627 (HRTO); *Audmax Inc. v. Ontario (Human Rights Tribunal)* [2011] 72 CHRR 315 (ONSC). See also Margaret Wente, "The case of the smelly lunch," *Globe and Mail*, 3 February 2011.

100 The commission also ordered the ministry to renovate two of its detention centres to accommodate morbidly obese prisoners. No author, "Quebec fined for not accommodating obese prisoner," *Toronto Star*, 29 September 2012. See also *Pivot Legal Society v. Downtown Vancouver Business Improvement Assn. (No. 6)* [2012] 73 CHRR 23 (BCHRT). See also Darryl Greer, "Drug Users & Homeless Seek Equal Rights," *Courthouse News Service*, 12 April 2012; Andrea Woo, "Homeless group set to sue Abbotsford for harassment," *Globe and Mail*, 24 July 2013.

101 The owner showed her the letter so that she could file a police complaint, which she followed with a complaint to the human rights commission. *Commission des droits de la personne et des droits de la jeunesse v Delisle* [2013] CHRR 17 (QCTDP).

102 Andrew Woo, "Federal heroin prohibitions violate B.C. patients' Charter rights, lawyer argues," *Globe and Mail*, 25 March 2014.

103 *Hicks v Human Resources and Skills Development Canada* (2013) CHRT 20.

104 Maryse Zeidler, "B.C. Mother files human rights complaint after shift change leaves her without daycare," *CBC News*, 30 June 2018.

105 *Citizens for Safe Technology v. BC Hydro* [2012] CHRR 200 (BCHRT). See also no author, "Human rights complaint against BC Hydro's smart meters approved by tribunal," *Toronto Star*, 2 September 2012.

106 *Thompson v. Display Potentials Inc.* [2012] CHRR 1386 (HRTO). See also Norman De Bono, "Fired 'soccer mom' seniors launch human rights battle," *Toronto Sun*, 20 August 2012.

107 Alex Butler, "City's Harm Reduction Ban Brings on Lawsuit," *Abbotsford News*, 23 May 2013.

108   *Williams v. Iroquois Falls (Town) (No. 2)* [2012] CHRR 1483 (HRTO).
See also Arminga Ligaya, "Human rights tribunal dismisses disabled man's
bid to have town pay for snow removal," *National Post*, 7 August 2012.

109   Renata D'Aliesio, "Fight to memorialize police PTSD victims goes to
Human Rights Tribunal," *Globe and Mail*, 20 December 2015.

110   Another debate is emerging over whether discrimination based on genetic
characteristics should be included in human rights legislation. This would
prohibit insurers and employers from discriminating based on genetic background—for instance, denying insurance to an individual with a genetic
marker that may lead to Huntington's disease. Theresa Boyle, "Genetic
discrimination by insurers under debate," *Toronto Star*, 18 May 2011;
Carly Weeks, "Health Insurance and 'Genetic Discrimination': Are Rules
Needed?" *Globe and Mail*, 1 January 2012; Keith Leslie, "Advocates back
Ontario bill aiming to safeguard genetic data from insurance firms," *Globe
and Mail*, 4 November 2013.

111   Ontario Human Rights Commission, *Annual Report 2017–2018* (Toronto:
Government of Ontario, 1996). bit.ly/2L5Rf3H.

112   Postmedia News, "Demanding a Facebook password a violation of human
rights: commission," *Times Colonist*, 23 March 2012.

113   Mark Evans, "Are Canadian Internet Uses Really 'Third World'?" *Forbes*,
14 September 2012.

114   Renters have filed human rights complaints because of neighbours who
smoked and in response to contentious evictions. No author, "Smoking
neighbour human-rights case moves forward in B.C.," *Alberni Valley
Times*, 12 August 2011; Mark Weisleder, "Pot-smoking tenant may be
hard to evict," *Toronto Star*, 2 December 2011; Alex Ballingall, "Should
Canada make adequate housing a human right?," *The Star*, 28 June 2018.

115   John Paul Tasker, "Trudeau says housing is a human right—what does that
mean exactly?" *CBC News*, 23 November 2017.

116   "A sad week for human rights in Canada," *National Union of Public and
General Employees Newsletter*, 18 March 2012; Sean Fine, "Top court
upholds Canadian workers' right to strike," *Globe and Mail*, 30 January
2015.

117   Canadian Press, "Bullying won't be human rights offence in Manitoba,"
5 September 2013.

118   David Suzuki, "Clean drinking water should be a human right in Canada,"
Georgia Straight, 25 November 2014.

119   Hamilton Health Sciences Corp. v D.H. [2014] ONCJ 603.

120   A year later, as government lawyers were preparing an appeal, the family
and judge agreed to a compromise that would allow the child to receive
both traditional medicine and chemotherapy. Kelly Grant, "Aboriginal girl
now receiving both chemo and traditional medicine," *Globe and Mail*, 24
April 2015.

121   Content Advisory Committee, *Final Report* (Winnipeg: Canadian Museum
for Human Rights, 2010).

122   On Twitter, see the following accounts at twitter.com: /susanneure, /gord
barnes, /write4justice, /hurtinalbertan, /jhcentre, /wavam, /amnestysecurity,
/aidslaw, /papershadow, /sgmlaw, /right2housing.

123 See, for instance, http://blog.freedomsite.org; http://scaramouchee
     .blogspot.ca; http://forlifeandfamily.blogspot.ca; http://canadianhuman
     rightscommission.blogspot.ca.

124 See, for example, http://blogs.united-church.ca/unwrappingdevelopment;
     http://bccla.org/our-work/blog; http://www.ccla.org/rightswatch.

125 See, for example, http://blogs.mcgill.ca/humanrightsinterns.

126 See, for example, http://www.canadaemploymenthumanrightslaw.com.

127 http://www.jhcentre.org/news-blog.

128 "EGALE and GALE BC celebrate safe schools victory: Final victory for
     bullied student sends message to schools across Canada" (2005), Egale
     Canada, retrieved 3 January 2012 from http://www.egale.ca/index
     .asp?lang=E&menu=1&item=1179. "A 'teachable moment': Human
     rights case underlines homophobia in schools" (2006), Egale Canada,
     retrieved 3 January 2012 from http://www.egale.ca/index.asp?lang
     =E&item=1321.

129 "Adding gender identity and gender expression to the *Human Rights
     Act* tells trans people that they can accept themselves and live in dig-
     nity free from discrimination and harassment." "About EGALE" (2011),
     Egale Canada, retrieved 3 January 2012 from http://www.egale.ca/index
     .asp?lang=E&menu=1&item=1152.

130 Steve Rennie, "Rival Métis groups from B.C. take feud to human-rights
     commission," *The Gazette* (Montreal), 16 June 2014.

131 "The United Nations Declaration on the Rights of Indigenous Peoples:
     What It Says and What It Means for First Nations in Canada" (2007),
     Assembly of First Nations, retrieved 3 January 2012 from http://www.afn
     .ca/uploads/files/07-12-4_un_declaration_flyer_fe.pdf.

132 Specifically, they want the federal government to legislate the right to clean
     and safe drinking water and sanitation. "Assembly of First Nations, Amnesty
     International and Council of Canadians urge political leaders to recognize
     the human right to water" (2011), Assembly of First Nations, retrieved 3 Jan-
     uary 2012 from http://www.afn.ca/index.php/en/news-media/latest-news/
     assembly-of-first-nations-amnesty-international-and-council-of-canadia.

133 Joyce Crone, "Enough is enough," *Waterloo Region Record*, 2 December
     2011. In another letter to the editor, the author argues that water is a
     human right that the government has an obligation to protect. No author,
     "The rights to our water," *This Week*, 28 April 2011; Karen Howlett,
     "Natives halt talks over mineral rights," *Globe and Mail*, 19 March 2008,
     A4; Union of B.C. Indian Chiefs, "UBCIC Submission to Standing Senate
     Committee on Aboriginal Peoples – Bill S-11," 9 February 2011, http://
     www.ubcic.bc.ca/files/PDF/UBCICSubmissiontoSenate_S11_020911.pdf.

134 "UBCIC Fully Supports the Musqueam & Calls on the BC Government to
     Protect Infant Remains," retrieved 4 September 2013, http://www.ubcic
     .bc.ca/News_Releases/UBCICNews05031201.html#axzz26k6z1x6w.

135 Aboriginal women represent less than 3 percent of the population but
     10 percent of female homicide victims; there were 582 reported cases of
     missing or murdered Aboriginal women between 2000 and 2010; and
     while a suspect is charged in 84 percent of murder cases in Canada, the
     figure is less than half that when the victim is an Aboriginal woman. Craig
     and Mark Kielburger, "Violence against aboriginal women is Canada's top
     human rights issue," *Vancouver Sun*, 19 November 2012.

136 "Support the Secwepemec Defenders" (2005), Ontario Coalition Against Poverty, retrieved 3 January 2012 from http://ocap.ca/node/701.

137 "Victory at Everest! Disabled Activist Receives Public Apology for Discrimination" (2008), Ontario Coalition Against Poverty, Retrieved 3 January 2012 from http://ocap.ca/node/1259.

138 "Filipinos Rally Against Deportations of LCP Workers" (2006), Ontario Coalition Against Poverty, retrieved 3 January 2012 from http://ocap.ca/node/535; "Solidarity Across Borders: Struggling for Justice And Dignity for Migrants and Refugees" (2004), Ontario Coalition Against Poverty, retrieved 3 January 2012 from http://ocap.ca/node/606.

139 Trish Garner, "Charity not correct way to tackle poverty in B.C.," *Vancouver Sun*, 12 January 2015. BC Poverty Reduction Coalition, "Poverty in BC is a Human Rights Violation," retrieved 3 February 2015 from http://bcpovertyreduction.ca/2014/12/poverty-in-bc-is-a-human-rights-violation.

140 Kendra Milne, *High Stakes: The Impacts of Child Care on the Human Rights of Women and Children* (Vancouver: West Coast LEAF, 2016).

141 "Ashley Smith's human rights were violated, advocate says," *CBC News*, 20 May 2013.

142 Council of Canadians with Disabilities: http://www.ccdonline.ca/en.

143 For the Canadian Association of the Deaf papers, visit http://www.cad.ca.

144 Canadian Council of Muslim Women, "Being a Canadian Muslim Woman in the 21st Century," 1 October 2010, http://ccmw.com/being-a-canadian-muslim-woman-in-the-21st-century.

145 For United Church position papers, visit http://www.united-church.ca.

146 For National Association of Women and the Law position papers, visit http://www.nawl.ca.

147 Young Women's Christian Association, "Confronting Violence Against Women" and "Upcoming Events," retrieved 4 September 2013 from http://ywcacanada.ca/en/pages/wwv/planning/confronting and http://ywcacanada.ca/en/events/96. Women Against Violence Against Women, "Urban Women's Anti-Violence Strategy," retrieved 4 September 2013 from http://www.wavaw.ca/campaigns/urban-womens-anti-violence-strategy.

148 "Anniversary of the Universal Declaration of Human Rights" (2002), Vancouver Rape Relief & Women's Shelter, retrieved 3 January 2012 from http://rapereliefshelter.bc.ca/learn/news/anniversary-universal-declaration-human-rights.

149 On women and rights discourse, see Dominique Clément, *Equality Deferred: Sex Discrimination and British Columbia's Human Rights State, 1953–1984* (Vancouver: UBC Press and the Osgoode Society for Canadian Legal History, 2014). On Aboriginal peoples and rights discourse, see Peter Kulchinsky, *Aboriginal Rights Are Not Human Rights* (Winnipeg: ARP Books, 2013); J.R. Miller, "Human Rights for Some: First Nations Rights in Twentieth-Century Canada," in *Taking Liberties: A History of Human Rights in Canada*, ed. Stephen Heathorn and David Goutor (Toronto: Oxford University Press, 2013).

150 Charles Beitz briefly explores this distinction. According to him, human rights should not be seen as defining a minimum standard, but neither should it be equated fully with social justice. He suggests that human rights are a subset of social justice that have priority over other claims based on

economic, social, political, and cultural context. Charles R. Beitz, *The Idea of Human Rights* (New York: Oxford University Press, 2009), 141–44.

151   There is no agreed-upon definition of social justice, as evinced by the expansive literature on theories of justice. To begin exploring some of the central debates around theories of justice, see Ronald Dworkin, *Sovereign Virtue: The Theory and Practice of Equality* (Cambridge, MA: Harvard University Press, 2000); Amartya Sen, *Development as Freedom* (New York: Random House, 2000); John Rawls, *A Theory of Justice* (New York: Oxford University Press, 1999).

152   A few recent studies on human rights have proffered a similar distinction between rights and social justice. For instance, as Nancy Hodgson points out, "a growing number of scholars, policy-makers, and activists have become increasingly wary of the dominance of rights-based approaches to social justice and, increasingly, development ... The demand of women (and men) in the global south for economic justice in the face of repeated efforts by states, elites and capital to alienate their land and undermine their livelihoods in the name of particular neoliberal visions of 'progress' and 'productivity' reveals the limits of legal frameworks for obtaining social justice. Part of the problem is that rights-based protocols empower states—the very entities most often accused of violating the rights of individuals and collectivities— ... to implement and enforce laws to protect their rights. But nation-states are far more likely to selectively enforce the rights of privileged individuals than to guarantee collective rights for groups, whether indigenous, minority or women." Dorothy L. Hodgson, ed., *Gender and Culture at the Limits of Rights* (Philadelphia: University of Pennsylvania Press, 2011), 1, 12. Similarly, as Charles Beitz explains, "one might be tempted to hold that human rights simply *are* the rights of social justice. This, however, cannot be right ... Human rights are matters of international concern and it is not plausible that the international community should take responsibility for the justice of its component societies. For one thing, requirements of justice are grounded in the interests of different degrees of urgency and therefore exert claims of different weights ... Secondly, some requirements of justice may not be achievable by means of any permissible form of action ... Finally, it is not unreasonable to expect the requirements of social justice, at the level of institutions, laws, and policies, to vary across societies in ways that respond to differences in the economic, social, and cultural background." Beitz, *The Idea of Human Rights*, 142–43.

153   James Griffin, *On Human Rights* (New York: Oxford University Press, 2008), 199.

154   Sen, *Development as Freedom*, 285.

155   Beitz, *The Idea of Human Rights*, 143.

156   Sen, *Development as Freedom*, 287–88.

157   Ibid.

158   Tanya Basok and Suzan Ilcan, *Issues in Social Justice: Citizenship and Transnational Struggles* (Toronto: Oxford University Press, 2013), 4.

159   Ibid.

160   Brian Barry, *Why Social Justice Matters* (Cambridge: Polity Press, 2005), 22.

161 *Moore v British Columbia (Education)* (2012) 3 SCR 360.

162 *First Nations Child and Family Caring Society of Canada et al. v. Attorney General of Canada (for the Minister of Indian and Northern Affairs Canada)* 2016 CHRT 2.

163 The *Moore* case, according to human rights lawyer Pearl Eliadis, established that "children who have dyslexia have a right to special education for the simple reason that all children have the right to receive public education in accordance with the law." Eliadis, *Speaking out on Human Rights*, 20.

164 See, for instance, ibid., 138–51; Gwen Brodsky, "Governments as Interpreters and Shapers of Human Rights," in *14 Arguments in Favour of Human Rights Institutions*, ed. Shealgh Day, Lucie Lamarche, and Ken Norman (Toronto: Irwin Law, 2014); Lucie Lamarche, "Economic and Social Rights in an Era of Globalization and Governance Arrangements in Canada: The Need to Re-Visit the Issue of the Implementation of International Human Rights Law," in *Is Our House in Order? Canada's Implementation of International Law*, ed. Chios Carmody (Montreal and Kingston: McGill–Queen's University Press, 2010).

165 William Schabas and Stéphane Beaulac, *International Human Rights and Canadian Law: Legal Commitment, Implementation and the Charter*, 3rd ed. (Toronto: Thomson Carswell, 2007). In 1987, Chief Justice Brian Dickson articulated a doctrine for how Canadian judges should use international law when interpreting the *Charter of Rights and Freedoms*. According to Dickson, judges can use international law when interpreting the Charter, but they are not bound by international law. It should be treated similar to comparative law rather than domestic law. "In short, though I do not believe the judiciary is bound by the norms of international law in interpreting the Charter, these norms provide a relevant and persuasive source for interpretation of the provisions of the Charter, especially when they arise out of Canada's international obligations under human rights conventions." *Reference Re. Public Service Employee Relations Act (Alta.)*, [1987] 1 S.C.R. 313.

166 See, for instance, Abdullahi Ahmed An-Na'im, ed., *Human Rights in Cross-Cultural Perspectives: A Quest for Consensus* (Pennsylvania: University of Pennsylvania Press, 1992); Jane K. Cowan, Marie-Bénédicte Dembour, and Richard A. Wilson, eds., *Culture and Rights: Anthropological Perspectives* (Cambridge: Cambridge University Press, 2001); Alison Brysk, ed., *Globalization and Human Rights* (Berkeley: University of California Press, 2002).

167 For a more detailed critique of international human rights law, see Posner, *The Twilight of Human Rights Law*. As Philip Alston pointed out in his 1984 essay on rights inflation, there is also the problem that new human rights have been proclaimed in the past without seeking the approval of the General Assembly. Instead, commissions within the United Nations have simply declared new human rights, even when they have been opposed by member nations. Philip Alston, "Conjuring Up New Human Rights: A Proposal for Quality Control." *American Journal of International Law* 78, no. 3 (1984): 607–21.

168 "The belief is widespread that human rights mark what is most important in morality; so whatever any group in society regards as most important, it will be strongly tempted to declare it to be a human right. The group will be out to annexe the force of the term for its own keenest concerns. It is now also a common, and not unjustified, belief that getting something widely accepted as a human right is a good first step to getting it made a legal right; so there is a great temptation to assert that anything to which one wants to have a legal guarantee is a human right. And getting something accepted as a human right transforms one's case. One is transformed from beggar ('you ought to help me') to chooser ('it is mine by right'). If one can claim by right, one is not dependent upon the grace or kindness or charity of others. These features of the discourse of human rights are responsible both for great good and great bad, the bad being the ballooning of the discourse itself." Griffin, *On Human Rights*, 92.

169 Ibid.

170 Even Amnesty International and Human Rights Watch, two organizations that resisted expanding their mandate beyond civil and political rights for most of their history, have surrendered to rights inflation. Amnesty International formally expanded its mandate in 2001 (Human Rights Watch in 2003) to include social and economic rights. Amnesty International now advocates for, among other issues, a human right to water for Aboriginal peoples in Canada. Of course, there is no doubting the legitimacy of such grievances. These are, to be sure, important social justice issues. What is significant is that Canadians are framing virtually every grievance as human rights, and they are using human rights law as a forum for redress. There are many implications of rights inflation, but the most alarming effect is the backlash it has enabled against our human rights legal system. Daniel Chong, "Economic Rights and Extreme Poverty: Moving Towards Subsistence," in *The International Struggle for New Human Rights*, edited by Clifford Bob, 108–29 (Philadelphia: University of Pennsylvania Press, 2009), 117–23

171 Ibid., 109–10.

172 In this case, the author is offering an example of how environmentalists can address their grievances through the Inter-American Human Rights System. Romina Picolotti and Jorge Daniel Taillant, "Environmental Advocacy and the Inter-American Human Rights System," in *Linking Human Rights and the Environment*, ed. Romina Picolotti and Jorge Daniel Taillant (Tucson: University of Arizona Press, 2003), 147.

173 Constitutional protection for environmental rights is notably absent in common law nations such as Canada, the United States, Australia, and the United Kingdom. Boyd also notes that in many jurisdictions, the right to a healthy environment is primarily symbolic or declaratory. In other words, such rights lack stringent enforcement mechanisms compared to other rights. David R. Boyd, *The Environmental Rights Revolution: A Global Study of Constitutions, Human Rights, and the Environment* (Vancouver: UBC Press, 2012). Mank and Smith offer a useful summary of Boyd's key findings: "Seventeen nations locate environmental rights alongside economic, social, and cultural rights; eleven nations classify them as general objectives; three nations outline them in the constitution's preamble; two

nations describe them as 'Collective Rights'; one nation describes them as 'new Rights and Guarantees'; one nation describes them as 'Public Rights'; and one nation includes them in the 'Charter for the Environment.' ... eighty-three constitutions require individuals to bear some responsibility for protecting the environment. Six national constitutions 'establish an individual duty to protect the environment but neither establish an individual right to a healthy environment nor impose environmental obligations upon the state.' ... Other constitutions include restrictions on the use of private property; clauses relating to zoning, budget, hazardous waste, and clean water; the 'rights of Nature'; and the rights of future generations. Some constitutions provide explicit enforceability. On the other hand, other constitutions explicitly prohibit the judicial enforcement of environmental rights ... First, seventy-eight out of the ninety-two nations with a constitutional right to a healthy environment have actually incorporated that right into national legislation. Second, constitutional provisions recognizing the right to a healthy environment have positively influenced environmental lawsuits. Third, 'procedural environmental rights—to information, participation in decision making, and access to justice—are almost universally recognized as complements to the substantive right to a healthy environment.' Fourth, Boyd finds that 'constitutional environmental rights are delivering many of the anticipated benefits and few of the potential drawbacks forecast by legal experts.' Bradford C. Mank and Suzanne Smith, "Rev. Of David R. Boyd, the Environmental Rights Revolution: A Global Study of Constitutions, Human Rights, and the Environment, UBC Press, 2012," *Human Rights Quarterly* 35, no. 4 (2013): 1024, 2038.

174 Sonia Cardenas, *Chains of Justice: The Global Rise of State Institutions for Human Rights* (Philadelphia: University of Pennsylvania Press, 2014).

175 As Stammers argues in his book on social movements and human rights, "the tendency to try to mediate the entirely of social relations through constructions of human rights may well serve to devalue and discredit them." Neil Stammers, *Human Rights and Social Movements* (London: Pluto Press, 2009), 235.

176 The distinction between policy and principle, and the tendency of judges to apply human rights principles to strike down policies designed by governments to have particular social impacts, is developed in Michael Mandel, *The Charter of Rights and the Legislation of Politics in Canada* (Toronto: Thompson Educational, 1994).

177 Stefan-Ludwig Hoffman, "Introduction," in *Human Rights in the Twentieth Century*, edited by Stefan-Ludwig Hoffman, 1–21 (Cambridge: Cambridge University Press, 2011), 84.

178 Aryeh Neier, "Social and Economic Rights: A Critique," *Human Rights Brief* 13, no. 2 (2006): 1–3.

179 One of the earliest and best-known explorations of how human rights are a pursuit for legal recognition of moral claims is H.L.A. Hart, "Are There Any Natural Rights," *Philisophical Review* 64, no. 2 (1955). See also "Are There Any Natural Rights?," in *Theories of Rights*, ed. Jeremy Waldron (New York: Oxford University Press, 1990). Similarly, Costas Douzinas is critical of the legalization of human rights, albeit he distinguishes between subjective and institutional rights rather than social justice

and human rights. Costas Douzinas, *The End of Human Rights: Critical Legal Thought at the Turn of the Century* (Oxford: Hart Publishers, 2000).

180 Costas Douzinas, "The Poverty of (Rights) Jurisprudence," in *Human Rights Law*, ed. Connor Gearty and Costas Douzinas, 56–78 (Cambridge: Cambridge University Press, 2012), 58. Similarly, as Alan Gewirth notes, there is a paradox between the idea of universal human rights and their dependence on particular legal rules for their enforcement. Alan Gewirth, "Why Rights Are Indispensable." *Mind 95*, no. 379 (1986): 329–44.

181 "When the identity associated with the notion of disability is prescribed by the social model of disability, as opposed to the medical model, the expansion of rights becomes the most appropriate public policy tool for addressing the issues person[s] with disabilities face. By extension, legal mobilization—as collective action based on those rights—becomes a more acceptable method of influencing public policy than it might be otherwise. Vanhala, *Making Rights a Reality?*, 106

182 Richard Ashby Wilson, "Tyrannosaurus Lex: The Anthropology of Human Rights and Transnational Law," in *The Practice of Human Rights: Tracking Law between the Global and the Local*, ed. Mark Goodale and Sally Engle Merry, 342–69 (Cambridge: Cambridge University Press, 2007), 352.

183 See, for instance, Mary Ann Glendon, *Rights Talk: The Impoverishment of Political Discourse* (New York: Free Press, 1991); Michael Mandel, *The Charter of Rights and the Legislation of Politics in Canada* (Toronto: Thompson Educational, 1994).

184 Chong, "Economic Rights and Extreme Poverty," 124–27. Vanhala offers a similar argument in the context of the disability movement: "When the identity associated with the notion of disability is prescribed by the social model of disability, as opposed to the previously existing medical model, the expansion of rights becomes the most appropriate public policy tool for addressing the issues that disabled persons face. By extension, legal mobilization—collective actions based on those rights—becomes an acceptable method of influencing public policy, and the likelihood that it will be used as such increases." Vanhala, *Making Rights a Reality?*, 63.

185 Hodgson, *Gender and Culture at the Limits of Rights*, 1, 12.

186 There is, in fact, a well-established scholarship expressing skepticism around the potential of human rights and the law to address systemic social problems. Sociologist Maxine Molyneux insists that there is a distinction between human rights principles and Latin American governments' human rights policies. She argues that human rights policies have failed to close the gap between rhetoric and the material realities of women's lives in Latin America. Legal scholar Judy Fudge's study of the impact of the *Charter of Rights and Freedoms* found that it placed women on the defensive, forcing them to adopt the language of equal rights to the detriment of feminist discourses about power. In another study of the law, Fudge and Harry Glasbeek argued that "human rights legislation protects people from discrimination on the basis of seemingly ineluctable categories such as sex, disability, race, religion, place of origin, and not on the basis of economic subordination which may be expressed through these legally recognized differences." Maxine Molyneux and Sian Lazar, *Doing the Rights Thing: Rights-Based Development and Latin American Ngos*

(London: ITDG, 2003); Maxine Molyneux and Shahra Razavi, *Gender, Justice, Development and Rights* (New York: United Nations Research Institute for Social Development, 2003); Judy Fudge and Harry Glasbeek, "The Politics of Rights: A Politics with Little Class," *Social and Legal Studies* 1, no. 1 (1992): 61.

187 Vanhala, *Making Rights a Reality?*, 134–36.

188 There is growing recognition among transnational feminist activists that framing violence against women as a human rights issue has privileged lawyers and legal expertise. While the human rights framework has succeeded in raising awareness of the issue, it has been less effective in addressing prevention and treatment. As a result, some advocates are framing violence against women as a health issue. Margaret E. Keck and Kathryn Sikkink, *Activists Beyond Borders: Advocacy Networks in International Politics* (Ithaca: Cornell University Press, 1998), 198. On rights discourse and legal mobilization, see Vanhala, *Making Rights a Reality?*

189 Dorothy L. Hodgson, "Introduction: Gender and Culture at the Limits of Rights," in *Gender and Culture at the Limits of Rights*, ed. Dorothy L. Hodgson (Philadelphia: University of Pennsylvania Press, 2011).

190 As Judy Fudge argues in her analysis of sexual assault laws in Canada, "instead of directly addressing the question of how to best promote women's sexual autonomy under social relations which result in women's sexual subordination, feminists who invoke the *Charter* must couch their arguments in terms of the rhetoric of equality rights ... feminist discourse about power is translated into a discourse of rights." Judy Fudge, "The Effect of Entrenching a Bill of Rights Upon Political Discourse: Feminist Demands and Sexual Violence in Canada," *International Journal of the Sociology of Law* 17, no. 4 (1989): 458–59.

191 Dorothy L. Hodgson draws a similar conclusion in the context of gender-based violence: "We need to be alert to the ways in which discourses about gender-based violence and the suffering of women create particular cultural and political subjects, which often accompany and can come to subvert some of the other powerful enabling ideas of human rights. Human Rights positions itself as a neutral field of equality for all. Such a claim of neutrality, however, denies the myriad ways in which ideas about what it means to be a woman, about the proper relations between men and women, about the existence of a private and a public sphere, for example, structure the demands and expectations of rights." Hodgson, "Introduction: Gender and Culture at the Limits of Rights."

192 Lori Chambers, "'In the Name of the Father': Children, Naming Practices, and the Law in Canada," *UBC Law Review* 43, no. 1 (2010–11); Wanda Wiegers, "Gender, Biology, and Third Party Custody Disputes," *Alberta Law Review* 47, no. 1 (2009); Fudge, "The Effect of Entrenching a Bill of Rights upon Political Discourse."

193 Aryeh Neier, *The International Human Rights Movement: A History* (Princeton: Princeton University Press, 2012), Chapter 3. In contrast, Kaletski and colleagues argue that constitutionalizing economic and social rights can lead to the "creation of rules, formal and informal, to which politicians must adhere. It can further potentially force policymakers to enact laws and regulations specifically aimed at improving the quality of

ESR fulfillment. This could include increasing expenditures and improving access to services for vulnerable populations." Their study, however, does not consider whether or not constitutionalizing these rights leads to effective legal enforcement. Elizabeth Kaletski et al., "Does Constitutionalizing Economic and Social Rights Promote Their Fulfillment?," *Journal of Human Rights* 15, no. 4 (2016): 434.

194 Posner, *The Twilight of Human Rights Law*, 89.

195 Chong, "Economic Rights and Extreme Poverty," 124–27.

196 As Wilson notes, the "legalization of rights is mystifying (in the historical materialist sense) insofar as it raises false expectations that the state can solve social and economic problems, and normalizing, insofar as it employs the legal/bureaucratic system but does not challenge it." Wilson, "Tyrannosaurus Lex," 352.

197 Rose Freedman and Jacob Mchangama, "Expanding or Diluting Human Rights?: The Proliferation of United Nations Special Procedures Mandates," *Human Rights Quarterly* 38, no. 1 (2016): 164–93.

198 For a more detailed discussion on human rights and war, see Posner, *The Twilight of Human Rights Law*, Chapter 6.

199 Clément, *Equality Deferred*. The human rights statutes of Saskatchewan and Alberta include references to fundamental freedoms, but have proven largely symbolic. The most comprehensive human rights statute in Canada is Quebec's *Charte des droits et libertés de la personne,* which includes economic and social rights. Yet, again, in practice the law has functioned primarily as an anti-discrimination statute and has done little to address systemic inequalities. Lucie Lamarche, *Le Régime Québécois De Protection Et De Promotion Des Droits De La Personne* (Montreal: Les Éditions Yvon Blais, 1996); Clément, *Equality Deferred*; Colleen Sheppard, "The Promise and Practice of Protecting Human Rights: Reflections on the Quebec *Charter of Human Rights and Freedoms,*" in *Mélanges,* ed. Paul-André Crépeau (Cowanville: Les Éditions Yvon Blais, 1997); R. Brian Howe and David Johnson, *Restraining Equality: Human Rights Commissions in Canada* (Toronto: University of Toronto Press, 2000).

200 Douzinas, "The Poverty of (Rights) Jurisprudence," 75.

201 Moreover, is there not a danger, as James Griffin, Beth Gaze, Melinda Jones, and many other have argued, that human rights is in danger of becoming a "debased rhetoric"? After an exhaustive study of developments in human rights law over the twentieth century, Gaze and Jones concluded that "the language of rights is used in so many circumstances, to defend so many lines of argument, that it is now a debased form of rhetoric." If poverty in itself is a human rights violation, then it creates the possibility that governments can use economic or social imperatives for limiting rights. Amy Gutmann warns human rights institutions and agencies that "proliferation of human rights to include rights that are not clearly necessary to protest the basic agency or needs or dignity of persons cheapens the purpose of human rights and correspondingly weakens the resolve of potential enforcers." Gutmann also points out that rights inflation makes it more difficult to achieve intercultural assent to an international rights regime, and advises human rights agencies and institution against trying to "proliferate human rights beyond what is necessary to protect persons

as purposive agents." Beth Gaze and Melinda Jones, *Law, Liberty and Australian Democracy* (Sydney: Law Book Company, 1990), 9. Michael Ignatieff, *Human Rights as Politics and Idolatry* (Princeton: Princeton University Press, 2001), x.

202 Griffin comes to a similar conclusion: "We have constantly to remind ourselves of the destructive modern tendency to turn all important moral matters into matters of rights, especially of human rights. We have to recover our sense of the power of the rest of our moral vocabulary ... We should be better off if we reserved talk about 'human rights' to a more restricted sense—and in that way gave it tolerably clear criteria for correct and incorrect use ... Once we recover a sense of the full range of our moral vocabulary, we shall no longer feel the need to turn all important moral claims into claims of rights. My personhood account is deflationary in three related ways. It supplies a ground for rejecting certain actual declarations of human rights. It tends to narrow the content of individual human rights. And it reduces the importance of human rights. None of these deflationary effects seems to me regrettable. Human rights cover only one special part of morality; there are very many highly important moral domains outside the domain of human rights: for example, certain considerations of justice and fairness, some forms of equality, and many cases of one person's cruelty to another." Griffin, *On Human Rights*, 92.

203 Sen, *Development as Freedom*. See also Amartya Sen *The Idea of Justice* (Cambridge: Belknap Press of Harvard University Press, 2009).

The Right Investment in Rights

Nathalie Des Rosiers

> *If human rights and harmonious relations between cultures*
> *are forms of the beautiful, then the State is a work of art that*
> *is never finished.*
>
> —F.R. Scott [1]

Professor Clément worries about rights inflation. He worries about the absence of limits on the use of the terms "rights" and "human rights" and the consequent loss of the "evocative power" of human rights. He worries that social justice claims are being framed as rights and that human rights commissions are engaging in complex redistributive allocations. He would limit "human rights" to freedom of religion, association, assembly, the press, and speech and the right to due process and equal treatment—matters in which, he asserts, a consensus about recognizing them was historically achieved.

I also worry. I worry that too many injustices remain hidden and silenced, that people are unable to exercise their right to vote, their right to speak, or their right to participate in society because of discrimination or poverty. I worry that discriminatory policing is infringing on basic due process rights. I worry that lack of accountability undermines the right to free speech or the right to peaceful assembly, and I worry that the failure to recognize socio-economic rights condemns women and marginalized groups to poverty and discrimination. I do not worry about having too many human rights, but rather about not having enough. I worry about lack of enforcement, but I do not attribute this lack of enforcement to the "cacophony" of rights, but rather to an entrenched resistance to the transformative power of rights.

So we speak from different places. Although Clément and I share many goals, including more equality and more social justice, we reach these goals differently.

Reading his essay reminded me of previous encounters when shared goals did not equate with shared intellectual views. In 1987 I participated in a joint session between political science and law on linguistic rights. I was a very young academic, as well as the only legal academic on the panel, and the discourse was very much about the role of law in the promotion and development of linguistic minorities in Canada: how law had failed francophone minorities; how law could depoliticize the issues and obscure past attempts to "assimilate" or "deny" the French fact in many provinces; and more generally how law had not succeeded in delivering what it sought to deliver.[2] It was a few years after the enactment of the *Constitution Act, 1982*,[3] and its Part I, the *Canadian Charter of Rights and Freedoms*,[4] which provides some protection for linguistic rights.[5] For a legal academic, the question was whether linguistic rights ought to be interpreted broadly or narrowly, as a "political compromise"[6] or as "fully fledged collective human rights."[7] Those were the questions that jurists ask. The sociologists, the political scientists, and the historians were more interested in the losses that rights talk would inflict on the political cause. They feared that lawyers were taking up too much space in the debate. Had Clément been there, he would have thought I was engaging in inflationary rhetoric, for I argued that minority linguistic rights could be understood as "human rights." The taxonomy that Clément presents here would frame linguistic rights as "fringe rights," outside the set of "core rights" he wishes to protect, and therefore as less legitimate than the core ones. He would view them as rights conferred on a minority as a political compromise that should be interpreted narrowly.

The meeting in 1987 ended well. We agreed that we both had a role to play: I would continue to advocate for a purposive and generous interpretation of linguistic rights, and they would continue to empower the community to take action and to stand up to government, to organize, to vote strategically in order to create a vibrant and dynamic Franco-Ontarian civil society.

Ironically, we met again around the Montfort Hospital closing in 1997 when the conservative Ontario government led by Premier Mike Harris wanted to rationalize health services and proposed the amalgamation of "l'Hôpital Montfort" with other Ottawa hospitals. Such restructuring would significantly diminish the role of l'Hôpital Montfort as a Franco-Ontarian institution able to provide services to the French community. There were protests[8] and, eventually, a court case. The Divisional Court overruled the findings of the Restructuring Commission,[9] but that victory for the Franco-Ontarian community was short-lived as the Ontario government appealed. The Ontario Court of Appeal did not recognize the right to health care in French,[10] but it did require the government to "consider" the impact on the francophone minority of the proposed restructuring. This court case provided an occasion for the French community to explain why institutions were essential to its survival and gave it the time and the opportunity to articulate its demands and to organize. The French community mobilized, and "l'hôpital Montfort" is still open. This does not mean that all French organizations or institutions are protected from closure or that budgetary reasons could not be advanced to cut French services: the Court of Appeal recently found that relocation of governmental services in a non-designated area under the *French Services Act* was not a violation of linguistic rights and took into consideration the governmental objective of financial savings.[11] Nevertheless, the Montfort episode is a good example of the combination of rights advocacy and social activism that led to better protection of a minority that had been historically ignored by the political process in Ontario.

I had a sense of déjà vu when I read Professor Clément's article. The debate between law skeptics and law enthusiasts has not died out over the past twenty years: this testifies to the vitality of academic debates about the instruments available and necessary for social change. Lawyers tend to think that politics alone, without the pressures of legal claims, will not deliver social justice, and sociologists and political scientists despair at the arrogance of rights discourse and its ineffectiveness in actually delivering social change. In a way, both are right.

My critique of Clément's "rights inflation" has two main parts. First, I argue that the debate about rights inflation is misplaced: it stems from an exaggeration of the dangers of "rights inflation" on politics and from a minimization of the dangers of limiting rights. In the second part, I propose a more "positive" framework for analyzing the proliferation of rights claims and make two claims: first, that rights talk can be empowering and transform relationships and the allocation of responsibilities; and second, that a rights framework brings accountability and enhances democratic governance.

My point is not that a cautionary approach towards rights, and law more generally, is not warranted, but rather that rights are one of the mechanisms available to promote social justice, or to resist and push back against anti-social-justice agendas. Rights evolution should not be thwarted by taxonomy debates that may counter and diminish meaningful political and legal advances for marginalized groups.

THE REAL ECONOMICS OF RIGHTS INFLATION

Clément is concerned about the law's ability to address systemic social problems. He suggests that we distinguish between social justice and human rights. Human rights, in his formulation, would mean a return to a narrower set of "human rights" derived from the *International Covenant on Civil and Political Rights*:[12] freedom of religion, freedom of expression, freedom of peaceful assembly, due process rights, and the right to equal treatment. I suggest that this concern stems from an exaggerated fear of the rigidity of legal institutions, and a lack of appreciation of the dangers of "stultifying" legal rights and remedies.

Inflationary Rhetoric

Much of Clément's discomfort stems from two aspects of rights analysis:

- The focus on individual stories distorts the more general and rational way in which decisions ought to be made; *and*
- Rights analysis prevents compromise.

I disagree with both of these claims. Clément uses the Jeffrey Moore case as an example of the dangers of an expanded rights analysis. In his view, a human rights tribunal was wrong to find discrimination in a context where budgetary cuts were applied in the field of education. He also argues that the tribunal should not have ordered the government to compensate the Moore family for the private education costs of their disabled son. He worries that the plight of disabled students is not helped by a decision that focuses on one child rather than the thousands who have been affected by budget cuts. He is concerned that the human rights tribunal did not engage fully with the very important debate over whether the educational system values ableism and responds poorly to disability. In *Moore*, the Supreme Court of Canada did not disturb the tribunal's finding that the budgetary cuts had been applied in a greater proportion to disabled students' programs than to other programs.[13] The Court did not endorse the sweeping remedy proposed by the human rights tribunal, instead leaving it to the province to reflect on the best way to ensure equality and equity in education. Some commentators would have wanted more from the Court and argued that it would be preferable to impose a mandatory monitoring program on the government, rather than leave it to families with disabled students to fight against the government.[14]

The *Moore* decision has not ended the debate, it has simply opened it up. It has also reframed it. As discussed in the second part of this commentary, "rights talk" provides an opportunity for minorities to be heard. It ensures that majorities do not ignore the impact of their policies on individuals and groups. A discussion of the treatment of disabled children in public education is enhanced by the recognition of a right to equality in education. It does not mean that all wishes will be met; it does, however, clarify that public bodies must pay attention to the impact of their decisions on all children and that costs cannot be reallocated without taking into account the impact of this on disabled children.

Human rights law is clear: there is a duty to accommodate, but only up to the point of undue hardship. In *Moore*, the court summarized the law as follows:

> To demonstrate *prima facie* discrimination, complainants are required to show that they have a characteristic protected from discrimination under the *Code*; that they experienced an adverse impact with respect to the service; and that the protected characteristic was a factor in the adverse impact. Once a *prima facie* case has been established, the burden shifts to the respondent to justify the conduct or practice, within the framework of the exemptions available under human rights statutes. If it cannot be justified, discrimination will be found to occur.[15]

Charter rights are similarly subject to limitations "justifiable in a free and democratic society."[16] No right is unlimited. Limitations can be imposed. Once a right is established, the burden shifts to the government to prove that denial of the right is warranted. In a way, the conversation is changed: parents of disabled children who had been ignored in the debates around budgetary cuts now have a voice. The government must justify its choice. Why should it not?

Clément's objection stems from the focus on the individual family: Why should the parents of Jeffrey Moore have been reimbursed out of the public purse for the private school fees they paid? Damages to individuals who have suffered discrimination or rights violations may appear to be an "unjust reward" because that money could have been invested in the public school system to respond to the needs of *all* disabled children. However, those damages are the incentive for people to take cases to court. They compensate for the courage it takes to sue the government.

Clément may be worried that human rights tribunals will make mistakes and protect claims in ways that undermine the government's budgetary capacity to respond to others. For Clément, giving human rights commissions the power to arbitrate on competing claims is worse than giving this power to civil servants or politicians. But this misses the point that Jeffrey Moore's parents could have taken a different approach to obtaining satisfaction. They could have taken their case to the media (they may have). The media can play a role in pressuring governments to respond to individual cases. Alternatively, the Moores could have turned to crowdsourcing to get people to fund Jeffrey's education. These strategies might have empowered them and might have forced a broader conversation about the treatment of disabled children in public education, just as the Court case has. Litigation is but one way to shine a light on a particular issue. The long-term outcomes of the litigation will be felt through a series of compromises, since the costs and uncertainty of litigation always act as a sobering mechanism for the afflicted parties. If the human rights tribunal had dismissed the case and found that there was no discrimination, and if the Supreme Court had failed to recognize such discrimination, disabled children would have been worse off. Many more Jeffrey Moores would have had to resort to private education or forgo their access to instruction. A finding of "no right" diminishes the accountability owed to disabled children's families.

The Moore case was not about the right to education; rather, it was about equal access to government services.[17] So it is not the best case to test the inflation-of-rights hypothesis. It does, though, highlight that the courts are willing to criticize budgetary decisions and infuse the process with concern for the affected parties. As Gwen Brodsky explains:

> It is a big relief that in *Moore*, the Supreme Court of Canada held that the service in question was general education, not special education, and that Jeffrey Moore was not confined to comparing the treatment accorded to him with the treatment accorded to other students with disabilities ... The complaint in most disability accommodation cases is not that the complainant was treated differently from members of another group, but rather that there has been a failure to take disability into account and effectively remove a barrier to inclusion ...

> The goal of accommodating persons with disabilities is not to address different treatment. Rather, it seeks to render services, including general public education, accessible to persons with disabilities, taking account of disability-related difference and making such adjustments to norms and practices as are reasonably possible.[18]

In summary, rights are never absolute, not in Canada, and not around the world. It is simply incorrect to suggest that human rights language is a language of absolutes or that it prevents compromise. The recognition of a legal claim forces the government to respond. Law forces timing. A judge must respond. She cannot ignore the claim, as politicians can. However, compromise is often achieved. The vast majority of cases settle out of court. Even if they do not, the result is often an invitation to further processes of inclusion. This evolution is positive. The alternative to recognizing a right would be a loss of our democratic ability to make decisions that take all interests into account. A lack of recognition of a right to equality in education would silence voices, and it would perpetuate the ableism that pervades the system.

Deflationary Pressures

The question that arises from reading Clément's essay is *why?* Why worry about people claiming a right to housing under the rubric of human rights as opposed to the rubric of social justice? The opposition to socio-economic rights is located squarely within the capitalist culture that refuses to acknowledge that a redistributive claim can be grounded in the recognition of the commonality of human experience. After all, human rights are the rights that belong to humans, *qua* humans. What is to be gained by denying legitimacy to claims for transgendered justice or disability rights in schools?

There are dangers in restricting "human rights" to the civil and political dimension and denying the importance of socio-economic rights. Equality jurisprudence forces an acknowledgment of socio-economic realities. Clément's wish for a return to "equal treatment" could be interpreted as a rejection of the right to substantive equality and as a plea for a return to "formal equality," which used to be the law in Canada.[19] Denying the possibility of evolution in human rights risks rendering them meaningless and disconnected from present-day realities. Human rights frozen in time will have no value since they will not speak to current issues. In order to protect the relative value of "human rights," as defined by Clément, we could end up assigning them no value at all in current political discussions. In her critique of Michael Ignatieff's minimalist approach to human rights,[20] Gara Lamarche explains how for advocates around the world the idea of choosing certain rights over others, of choosing "political and civil rights" over socio-economic ones, renders the whole enterprise meaningless.[21] A hierarchy of rights, with civil and political rights at the top and socio-economic rights at the bottom, simply reinforces a Western model of rights discourse. I would argue that it reinforces a patriarchal model of rights where redistributive claims for newer voices (women, disabled students, transgendered people) are dismissed as "less important."

I also posit that the claim that there is growing ambivalence among Canadians about human rights is contradicted by the fact that more and more Canadians are using human rights language to frame their grievances. It could be that *some* Canadians are ambivalent or worried about the expansion of rights they do not support. Others want an expanded legal toolkit that reflects current issues. At the end of the day, the terrain of rights is always highly conflicted and will continue to be so. This reflects genuine differences regarding the common good and the proper way to resolve complex social issues. Rights advocacy is a necessary disputed terrain in a democracy—terrain that complements other avenues for resolving social claims.

I suggest below that a failure to support a "rights" language relevant to society's current issues undermines the capacity of a democracy to respond adequately. When a democracy is committed to the rule of law, it must give itself the legal ability to support claims—an ability rooted in part in legal language that is not, I repeat, a language of absolutes.

INVESTING IN RIGHTS

In this part, I present a vision of rights as instruments of democratization that foster and support the addition of new voices to a polity, and that increase accountability.

The Rights Voice Is the Right Voice

Starving and poor people may have the right to free speech, but their ability to be heard is limited. They are invisible. They are often ignored in a majoritarian democracy. Their struggle for survival is compounded by their lack of participation in elections, in the marketplace of ideas, and in public discussions. To grant them political rights without food, without housing, without medicine, and without education hardly responds to the complexity of their situation.

There is an overlap between social justice claims and human rights claims. The debate is whether it is better to restrict socioeconomic claims or collective rights to the rubric of social justice claims as argued by Clément, or to allow such claims to be framed as human rights. It is fundamental that the ways in which inequality is lived must be voiced. I argue that the ability to frame one's lived injustice as a violation of rights and a claim for equality is a sign of resilience. The evolution of human rights has been about allowing previously oppressed people to join in and leverage rights claims to build a society that is less discriminatory. There is no loss in having human rights law evolve and recognize transgendered oppression, new forms of disabilities, the intersection of multiple forms of discrimination, and the way in which poverty depletes the capacity to enjoy political rights, be it the right to expression, the right to vote, or the right to due process. Indeed, I argue that there is value in this evolution.

Every struggle can be framed differently than as rights-based: one could argue that women gaining the right to vote was not about human rights but rather about enhanced democracy and legitimacy, or that women's ability to sit on corporate boards is about enriched decision-making and not gender equality. That said, there is a profoundly important symbolic dimension to claiming a right to equality or a right to vote, rather than enhanced benefits for society. Let me provide a different example. Human rights talk has replaced "charitable" or religious talk as a means to redistribute income. With a decline in religious practice in the West, it is entirely appropriate that claims to support the poor and marginalized are being couched in legal rather than religious obligations. Indeed, the ability to frame one's demand for food in human rights language (the right to food, or the right to human dignity) instead of asking for charity places one in a position of symbolic equality vis-à-vis the provider. Requesting charity does not have the same empowering potential as claiming a right to human dignity. Indeed, when charitable and religious institutions were solely in charge of providing care to the poor and marginalized, their contributions were often linked to judgmental assessments of the religiosity or morality of the recipient. "Loose" women could not receive the same support as widows and were often required to "repent" before they were given health care or housing. Human rights claims are empowering because they cannot be ignored or delayed and are not conditional on being a "good person": they are universal and belong to all human beings.

To maintain its relevance and use for democracies, human rights language must speak directly to poverty, to security, and to collective issues.

For example, human rights have evolved to the point that they now encompass collective rights, such as self-determination for Indigenous peoples, linguistic rights, and even the right to a healthy environment. As a consequence, groups are able to make legal claims to empowerment. Rights discourse has become less abstract and more relevant. It is a positive development that freedom of association now recognizes the right to strike, that linguistic rights recognize the right to control educational institutions, that Indigenous rights recognize the right to protect ancestral lands for future generations. All of this provokes different conversations that speak directly to the power imbalance between employers and unions, majoritarian language holders and minorities, and colonizers and colonized. Legal claims do not supersede political or moral claims; they *support* those claims.

To the extent that there is a consensus that "civil and political" rights must be protected, that consensus was achieved at a time when women and other politically marginalized groups were less present. Rights talk is expanding today, and it is increasingly recognized that socio-economic rights are legitimate human rights. Both these developments are grounded in a movement to allow less powerful people to claim the law and to ask legal institutions to respond to their plight. There are many approaches that parents of a disabled child whose plight is ignored could take: they could go to the newspapers or to their provincial Parliamentarian, or they could ask a celebrity to endorse their cause. All of these avenues, if successful, may provide relief to the individual family and highlight the plight of disabled children in the education system, just as the legal system did. Why deny this family the ability to approach the courts?

The popularity of human rights talk resides in its power to transform: the voice can no longer be silenced. At times, it can force a reallocation of power. Legal claims cannot be ignored, they must be responded to. The process is often slow, but there will eventually be an answer. By contrast, the political process need not acknowledge that same voice unless it generates widespread public support or threatens social or economic stability. Some voices—gays and lesbians in earlier times, ethnic minorities, prisoners, non-citizens—have trouble being heard in the corridors of political power. Legal language often amplifies those voices so that they must be heard. Ultimately, then, human rights improves governance.[22]

Rights and Good Governance

Clément claims that the recent attacks on the human rights system are the result of rights inflation and of the error of expanding rights language beyond the "core" rights. Let me suggest a different diagnosis: human rights and equality regimes are always being attacked. Human rights tribunals and rulings were challenged vehemently in the 1960s because they challenged property rights. They were challenged in 1980s because they often challenged sexist practices. In the 1990s, racist, homophobic, and "ableist" assumptions were challenged, and the twenty-first century may be the time to expose the plight of Indigenous people and of transgendered people around the world.

Rights talk makes it possible to test the assumptions behind a decision. Is it true that order in a society requires that only heterosexuals marry? Is it true that no education system can be designed to better support access to education for disabled children? Courts are often a forum for testing whether governmental decisions are grounded in evidence and facts. I contend that the prospect of having to respond to legal challenges leads to better decision-making. The questions asked by a court require evidence-based decision-making.

To justify a potential infringement of a Charter right, the government must prove that its choices are reasonable in a free and democratic society. The government must prove that it has a legitimate objective, that its policy choice is rationally connected to this objective, and that the negative impact on the rights of the persons affected is proportional to the benefit for society. This analysis suggests that the government must conduct studies to ascertain the potential impact of its choices. In order to win, the government must prove that it has acted "rationally." It does not have to be absolutely right, but it must be making a reasonable choice between alternatives. This "rationality" analysis is central to the constitutional theory of rights in Canada: it dominates not only the legal but also the political forum. In Parliament, or in legislatures, elected politicians can and should ask about the basis for policy choices. The possibility that this choice could be challenged forces greater scrutiny of the evidence supporting the choice. In my view, this "right to rationality" enhances our democracy.[23]

Human rights law uses different language but strikes a similar balance between individual complaints about right violations and public good rationales. In the human rights context, individuals must be accommodated to the point of "undue hardship." This provides an opening for employers, governments, or service providers to explain why they must say "no" to the accommodation requested by a disabled person, a religious minority member, or a woman.

Indeed, the metaphor of a "dialogue" between the legislative and judicial powers has come to dominate our understanding of institutional roles in the context of the *Canadian Charter of Rights and Freedoms*. It explains how the legislative and judicial powers interact: when the judicial power strikes down a statute, it gives the legislative power the opportunity to re-evaluate the situation and provide a new solution or a more convincing evidentiary basis for its legislative intervention, or to re-enact the same statute with the use of the "notwithstanding clause" (Article 33 of the Charter). At times, courts have bowed to Parliament's wishes and have upheld the constitutionality of provisions previously identified as suspect.[24] The dialogue metaphor suggests that courts raise questions about the impact of legislative choices on individuals or groups and that the legislatures or Parliament, informed by this questioning, are the ultimate decision-makers. The legal forum, while not always ideal for assessing multifaceted decisions, works as a framing exercise. It is never the last word on the subject.

Current legal scholarship aims to link rights talk with institutional accountability[25]—that is, it is not content to simply assert a right, but wishes to connect it to a larger systemic response that must be developed. It is no surprise that human rights-based advocacy claims more exigent and stronger accountability mechanisms within bureaucracies, not only in courtrooms. In my view, we should move towards having a *right* to a privacy commissioner, a *right* to oversight in policing, and a *right* to an electoral watchdog. Future debates will no doubt raise these questions.

CONCLUSION

"Rights inflation" has a negative connotation. It suggests that people who frame their injustices as claims to rights are usurping or misappropriating other people's language. I have argued that in fact, the expansion of human rights to a range of new claims is a natural democratic movement. People should demand more of their governments and strive to eliminate discrimination and suffering. They can do so in a multitude of ways: by electing socially minded governments, but also by trying to protect certain values through legal means. Legal institutions must be part of the struggle for social justice. They are, however, but one avenue for addressing injustice.

Human rights law was about creating the possibility for people to want more than what they had, and about creating a more equal society that would ensure dignity for all. In this chapter I began by arguing that using the word "inflation" to describe the normal evolution of human rights is improper. Then in the first part, I suggested that Clément exaggerates the danger of rights claims for good public decision-making, and in the second part, I submitted that he underestimates the empowering nature of rights talk and the democratic contribution that rights can make.

I prefer to speak in terms of *investing* in human rights rather than viewing them as a threat. Human rights are never stagnant: they are a vehicle to claim better social justice. Once empowered, human beings want more justice. Human rights language will continue to adapt to new claims and to the possibility that different injustices ought to be highlighted and remedied. There is nothing menacing about this for our democracies. Indeed, as F.R. Scott suggests, "the State is a work of art that is never finished," and human rights are one of the tools that should be used to carve or paint a better and a most just future.

Notes

1 Cited in John Robert Colombo, *Famous Lasting Words—Great Canadian Quotations* (Toronto, Douglas & McIntyre, 2000), 462.

2 See the resulting book from the exchanges: Linda Cardinal, ed. *Une Langue qui pense : la recherche en milieu minoritaire francophone au Canada* (Ottawa: Presses de l'Université d'Ottawa, 1993).

3 Enacted as Schedule B to the *Canada Act 1982*, 1982, c. 11 (U.K.), which came into force on 17 April 1982.

4 http://laws-lois.justice.gc.ca/eng/Const/page-15.html#h-38.

5 Sections 16 to 23 provide protection to linguistic rights: it establishes that French and English are the official languages of Canada (sect. 16), the right to speak and be served by the government in the official language of one's choice (sect. 20), as well as a limited right to have one's children educated in the official language of one's choice (sect. 23).

6 This language comes from the opinion of Justice Beetz in *Société des Acadiens du Nouveau-Brunswick Inc. v. Association of Parents for Fairness in Education*, [1986] 1 S.C.R. 549, para. 64.

7 This purposive interpretation was later affirmed in *R. v. Beaulac*, [1999] 1 S.C.R. 768.

8   Robert Yergeau describes the process in this way (TRAD): "from popular demonstrations to internet conversations, from proposed limits on the closure to lobbying, from reluctant acceptance by the government, to eventually great disappointment," in Roger Bernard, À la défense de Montfort (Sudbury: Prise de parole, 2000).

9   *Lalonde v. Ontario (Commission de restructuration des services de santé)* 48 OR (3d) 50; 181 DLR (4th) 263; [1999] OJ No 4488 (QL); Citation:), 1999 CanLII 19910 (ON SC), http://canlii.ca/t/g1grn, retrieved 14 December 2015.

10 *Lalonde v. Ontario (Commission de restructuration des services de santé)* (2001), 56 O.R. (3d) 505, [2001] O.J. No. 4768 (C.A.).

11 *Giroux v. Ontario*, 75 OR (3d) 759; [2005] OJ No 2569 (QL); 199 OAC 153.

12 http://www.ohchr.org/en/professionalinterest/pages/ccpr.aspx.

13 *Moore v. British Columbia (Education)*, 2012 SCC 61.

14 See Joanna Birenbaum and Kelly Gallagher Mackay, *From Equal Access to Individual Exit: The Invisibility of Systemic Discrimination in Moore* (June 25, 2013), 10 *Journal of Law & Equality*, 93–112, 2013. Available at SSRN: http://ssrn.com/abstract=2284865.

15 *Moore v. B.C., supra*, note para. 33.

16 Section 1 of the *Charter* states: "The Canadian Charter of Rights and Freedoms guarantees the rights and freedoms set out in it *subject only to such reasonable limits prescribed by law as can be demonstrably justified in a free and democratic society.*"

17 Bruce Ryder, Cidalia C Faria, & Emily Lawrence, "What's Law Good For? An Empirical Overview of Charter Equality Rights Decisions" (2004) 24 Sup Ct L Rev 103; Bruce Ryder & Taufiq Hashmani, "Managing Charter Equality Rights: The Supreme Court of Canada's Disposition of Leave to Appeal Applications in Section 15 Cases, 1989–2010" (2010) 51 Sup Ct L Rev 505.

18 Gwen Brodsky, "*Moore v British Columbia: Supreme Court of Canada Keeps the Duty to Accommodate Strong*" (2013) 10 J.L. & Equal. 85, at 89–91.

19 See for a description of the evolution of equality jurisprudence, among others, Jennifer Koshan and Jonnette Watson Hamilton, "The continual reinvention of section 15 of the Charter," (2013) 19 *University of New Brunswick Law Journal* 64.

20 Ignatieff, *Human Rights as Politics and Idolatry.*

21 Gara Lamarche, http://prospect.org/article/human-rights-politics-and -idolatry-michael-ignatieff.

22 For an exploration of the idea that aligning public policy with legal obligations leads to good governance outcomes, see Nathalie Des Rosiers, « L'État néolibéral, son environnement juridique et les cultures de transparence et d'imputabilité: une étude de l'écosystème canadien, » *Revue générale de droit* 36, no. 4 (2006): 543–60.

23 Nathalie Des Rosiers, « Réflexions critiques sur les implications de la « fraternité » in Michel Morin, Marie-Claire Cordonier Segger, Fabien Gélinas and Markus Gehring, eds., *Responsibility, Fraternity and Sustainability in Law – In memory of the honourable Charles Doherty Gonthier //*

Responsabilité, fraternité et développement durable en droit – en mémoire de l'honorable Charles Doherty Gonthier (Lexis Nexis, [2012]), 493–508.

24 The classical example is *R. v. Mills*, [1999] 3 S.C.R. 668, where the court upheld the rape-shield provisions of the *Criminal Code* previously struck down. The summary of the decision explains the Court's position in the following terms: "A posture of respect towards Parliament has been adopted by the courts. The relationship between the courts and the legislature should be one of dialogue. The courts do not hold a monopoly on the protection and promotion of rights and freedoms."

25 Nathalie Des Rosiers, « Pour une Charte de bonne gouvernance publique » (Hors série 2015) *Revue québécoise de droit international*, 171–82.

Too Many Rights?

Pearl Eliadis

Emperor:	Well, Herr Mozart! A good effort. Decidedly that. An excellent effort …
Mozart:	So then you like it? You really like it, Your Majesty?
Emperor:	Of course I do. It's very good. Of course, now and then—just now and then—it gets a touch elaborate.
Mozart:	What do you mean, Sire?
Emperor:	Well, I mean occasionally it seems to have, how shall one say?

[He stops in difficulty; turning to Orsini-Rosenberg]

Emperor:	How shall one say, Director?
Orsini-Rosenberg:	Too many notes, Your Majesty?
Emperor:	Exactly. Very well put. Too many notes.
Mozart:	I don't understand. There are just as many notes, Majesty, as are required. Neither more nor less.
Emperor:	My dear fellow, there are in fact only so many notes the ear can hear in the course of an evening … Don't take it too hard. Your work is ingenious. It's quality work. And there are simply too many notes, that's all. Cut a few and it will be perfect.

> *Mozart*:   Which few did you have in mind, Majesty?
>
> *Emperor*:   Well. There it is.
>
> —Peter Schaffer, *Amadeus* (1979)

INTRODUCTION

People regularly use rights language to both defend and attack the growing number of claims about what can or should count as a right.[1] This rapidly expanding catalogue of rights has generated concern about "too many rights" and "rights inflation,"[2] not only from progressive writers like Dominique Clément, but also from others who complain that the proliferation of rights has made human rights less relevant, contributing to their decline.[3] As a result, the legitimacy and effectiveness of human rights writ large is called into question.

This chapter argues that none of these concerns withstand scrutiny. In my 2014 book *Speaking Out on Human Rights: Debating Canada's Human Rights System* (discussed in more detail below), I examined the arguments for and against rights inflation in the Canadian context.

Contrary to what is argued by those who claim that human rights are suffering from rights inflation, the research discussed in *Speaking Out* points to an increase in the relevance of human rights, relying in part on quantitative information showing that the number of complaints filed since the 1980s has actually increased.[4] This research also reflects two qualitative factors that have increased the relevance of human rights: first, the extension of human rights concepts and law to people previously excluded from the rule of law, and second, the flexible and evolutionary development of human rights law and systems to meet the demands of rapidly changing societies. The findings show the adaptability of human rights as a body of law and its ongoing capacity to pull inchoate concepts of justice out of the chaos of their facts and organize them into cogent claims for justice based on human rights principles.

One of the critiques raised by Clément concerns the blurred distinction between categories of human rights he considers to be properly justiciable and other broad "social justice" claims that, in his view, should not be enforceable before the courts. Yet it is trite law—fundamental to any justice system worthy of its name—that any right must have a corresponding remedy. Economic, social, and cultural rights have been perceived by traditional civil libertarians like Alan Borovoy in Canada and Aryeh Neier in the United States as evidence of an undue expansion of human rights. Connected to this argument is the claim, made by authors like Eric Posner, that widespread global human rights violations are proof positive that human rights and the legal systems enforcing them do not have the capacity to meet expectations.

It is troubling that we never ask of other areas of law that which is demanded of human rights. No one argues, for example, that we should suppress new forms of intellectual property or restrict their development based on rights that may have existed a half-century ago. It would beggar belief to suggest that the many criminal cases before the courts constitute "proof" that criminal law has failed and is superfluous. It is equally troubling that the too-many-rights argument refutes the idea that rights should evolve to ensure that human rights law can address a wider cross-section of humanity and a more complete range of situations in which people should be able to access justice.

Access to justice and simplicity in the law are important objectives, but both law and the societies it regulates are increasingly complex. No one—not even specialists such as criminal or tax lawyers—knows everything there is to know about criminal or tax law, but neither branch of law has thereby been rendered less relevant.

Such arguments are made routinely in the arena of human rights law, and some of them hold considerable sway. The question is, Why?

One obvious response is that human rights law is more vulnerable because it is inherently, inevitably, and often explicitly political; human rights law pushes back against established authority (usually the state but also other powerful institutions and interests such as transnational corporations and corporate media), forcing concessions that would never otherwise be made. The reality of how rights emerge and the process by which human rights law comes to grips with changing norms may be less startling than attention-grabbing headlines about rights inflation intended to suggest that a crisis is at hand.[5] The iterative development of human rights suggests that we have been witness to more of a rights *evolution* than a rights *revolution*.

An informed inquiry about that evolution demands more than simply counting the number of existing rights or making bald comparisons between the rights we had at some arbitrarily designated point in time and those we have now. The idea that we have too many rights and are thereby diluting the value of "real rights" fails to recognize how we reformulate, reiterate, and modify established norms to protect those who have been excluded from the protection of law. Implicit in the "too many rights" approach is the notion that "real rights" should stay fixed and frozen at some arbitrary point in time. The Supreme Court of Canada perhaps said it best when rejecting "frozen concepts" of law:

> the "frozen concepts" reasoning runs contrary to one of the most fundamental principles of Canadian constitutional interpretation: that our Constitution is a living tree which, by way of progressive interpretation, accommodates and addresses the realities of modern life.[6]

In short, far from being an irrational or ideological expansion of claims leading to an overall devaluation of the currency of rights, the evolution of human rights has ensured that law can address new contexts and reach people excluded from the supposedly universal reach of rights because of their differences and particularities. As a result, rather than decreasing, the value and relevance of rights has *increased*.

The research presented in *Speaking Out* also shows that in Canada today, the ceiling on monetary awards has been raised substantially in jurisdictions where human rights systems have been reformed (as in Ontario, for example). Successful claims before courts and human rights tribunals have generated investments in more inclusive programs and institutions. The outcomes have created an effect that is precisely opposite to inflation, pointing to the greater value we place on freedom, equality, and human dignity for all people.

The increased value attributed to human rights has had real and practical consequences that have materially improved people's lives:

- *Refugee determination.* Refugee claimants in Canada have the right to an oral hearing to present their case and to understand the case against them.[7]

- *Women's rights in the workforce.* Women cannot be excluded from jobs by rules and practices that have nothing to do with legitimate occupational requirements.[8] Women also have the right to be free from sexual harassment and employers are liable for sexual harassment in the workplace.[9]

- *Equality for people of faith.* Religious beliefs and observances should be facilitated by offering reasonable accommodations at work and in educational institutions.[10]

- *Educational institutions.* All children, including children with learning disabilities, have the right to receive public education in accordance with the law.[11]

- *Health care.* People with disabilities have the right to adapted services in the health care system.[12]

- *Legislature.* LGBT people have the right to a human rights system that specifically prohibits discrimination against them, even in jurisdictions where the legislature has refused to extend human rights protection to LGBT people.[13]

- *End-of-life care.* People who have grave and irremediable medical conditions have the right to seek the assistance of physicians in dying.[14]

These and similar developments are cumulative and iterative and have resulted in fundamental social changes in Canada.

It is true that the rhetorical rut of Cold War thinking continues to divide civil and political rights from economic and social rights. This divide may be crumbling in many countries, and it has almost completely dissolved in international law, but it still represents a challenge in some countries, including Canada. Nestled in the divide is the dangerous idea that a core group of civil liberties can and should trump other rights. The idea relies on a hierarchy of rights separating justiciable "negative" rights or civil liberties from vague aspirations to social justice, which require a form of positive action by the state. The following section looks at this issue a little more closely.

WHAT IS MEANT BY "HUMAN RIGHTS"?

It is worth taking a minute to clarify what is meant by human rights as discussed in this chapter. The rights accorded to us due to our shared humanity are postulated as a catalogue of legally backed claims, which reflect our evolving understanding of human flourishing.[15] It is admittedly more difficult to engage with this more flexible, socially oriented idea of human rights than with frozen concepts of constitutional interpretation or one-dimensional understandings of rights. This evolutionary and dynamic conception is much more difficult than binary concepts of rights, which characterize claims as justiciable or not, individually framed or not, negative or positive, and so on.

Human rights law provides us with a responsive, normative, and open system or architecture that shapes, protects, and constrains human societies, with a special focus on the most vulnerable among us. As components of a fluid and open-ended legal system, human rights laws must and do evolve. However, individuals, collectives, and communities often struggle to use political and legal discourse to achieve the formal stability, predictability, and normativity of law. Although litigation is but one of many tools in a legal system, it is a fundamental one, at least in a country with a functioning judicial system and respect for the rule of law. Rights go hand in hand with social justice and require remedies in order to be meaningful.

TOO MANY NOTES?

The "too many notes" critique is powerful because it is easy to understand and hard to refute without elucidating the very complexity at which the critique points. The right to nationality is a good example. The underlying principle that people should have a nationality can be found in the 1948 *Universal Declaration of Human Rights* (the "Declaration") and the 1966 *International Covenant on Civil and Political Rights* (ICCPR).[16] In addition, however, in the 1990 *Convention on the Rights of the Child* (CRC) there is now a specific right granted to *a child* that has created an obligation on the state to register the nationality of a child at birth.[17] The CRC states that every child has the right to a nationality *and to be registered at birth*. This latter dimension is new, in the sense that it was not contained in earlier instruments, and it engenders state obligations as a necessary consequence of the general right to nationality.

In addition, specific and unique rights are granted to children of migrant workers under yet another instrument that addresses the particular circumstances of migrant workers who have children in a country other than their own.[18] When considered through a gender equality lens, nationality takes on other features, each of which requires a distinct response. Article 9 of the *Convention on the Elimination of All Forms of Discrimination against Women* prevents the discrimination inherent in the loss of nationality that occurs in some countries when women marry the nationals of other countries.[19] This is a distinct and unique right for women because it is usually married women who lose their national status and are therefore unable to convey their status to their children.

It would be easy to dismiss the subsequent iterations of nationality rights as "new rights" or as expansionist and inflationary. Closer inspection reveals that they are, in some respects, modifications of a single, basic right, one that has evolved for people whose circumstances require an explicit rendering of exactly what the original right means in practice. By characterizing this rendering as "inflation," we fail to appreciate the many dimensions in which rights are expressed and the new features of rights that emerge to address the circumstances of people who would otherwise lack protection.

Another example is the right to access the Internet. The expansion of human rights law to include the Internet is fundamental to freedom of expression as guaranteed in the ICCPR. The United Nations Special Rapporteur on the Promotion and Protection of the Right to Freedom of Opinion and Expression issued a report in 2011, noting that when governments crack down on political dissent, they often do so by banning access to the Internet, thereby violating fundamental freedoms. As remarked in the report, "the Special Rapporteur calls upon all states to ensure that Internet access is maintained at all times, including during times of political unrest."[20] It is ironic to hear critics—especially the media and civil libertarians—attacking this development, when connectivity is so important to the fundamental freedoms these groups claim as vital to a functioning democracy. Journalists, political activists, and bloggers rely heavily on the Internet to communicate with one another, expose corruption, substantiate human rights violations, and generate solidarity and support for their work. Internet blackouts are attractive to dictators and despots and are dangerous for human rights activists and journalists.

The rights evolution has another important feature alluded to earlier: it extends rights to people who were previously denied protection. In so doing, it has changed the contours and even the content of human rights. Despite human rights' universal aspirations, they have not always applied to all human beings. Women have battled for decades to have their rights recognized as human rights. According to human rights advocate David Baker, the rights of people with disabilities were not even discussed as a category of "human rights" until the 1980s.[21] Indigenous people have been denied the franchise, legal rights, and a host of civil, political, cultural, and social rights for decades in Canada. These are not historical phenomena of the distant past; it was only in 2008 that Indigenous people living on reserve were allowed to file human rights claims under the *Canadian Human Rights Act*.[22]

The extension of rights to different groups of people has taken place in a more or less sequential fashion. In anti-discrimination law, this sequencing is evident in the progression made since the earliest Canadian statutes, which contained only a limited number of grounds, such as race, colour, and religion. The current list of protected grounds is now more complete and includes disability, sex, age, ethnic origin, national origin, citizenship, and family status, among others. The right to be free from discrimination is entrenched in most human rights law statutes in Canada today. More recent additions to the grounds protected by human rights laws include sexual orientation and gender identity.

It is important to note that even those rights that may be considered "new rights" are no less legitimate by virtue of their more recent establishment in law. The courts did not recognize sexual harassment as a form of sexual discrimination until 1989.[23] Incredibly, British Columbia did not include the sexual harassment of tenants by a property manager as a form of discrimination until as late as 2012.[24] Some may view the right to equality on grounds of sexual orientation as a new right; however, litigants in cases like *Vriend* argued successfully that it is simply the natural extension of the right to equality for a specific group of human beings.[25] Gays and lesbians have a right to be free from discrimination, yet this right was not enshrined in the first or even the second, wave of human rights laws established in Canada. It is only very recently that trans people have been able to claim comparable rights, and their struggle is ongoing.

One of the most striking "new rights," resulting from the Supreme Court of Canada's decision in *Carter* in 2015, is the right to physician-assisted death.[26] *Carter* marks a significant departure from the Supreme Court of Canada's 1993 *Rodriguez* ruling, which had emphasized the "sanctity of life" as underpinning the constitutionality of the criminal prohibition on suicide. Two decades later, in *Carter*, the Court reinterpreted the right to life, liberty, and security of the person in the *Canadian Charter of Rights and Freedoms* (the "Charter") in a new matrix of fact and law and overturned its own previous ruling. It created the right to physician-assisted death under specific circumstances, albeit that right was fashioned from established Charter rights.[27]

The *Carter* case clarifies that the right to life, liberty, and security of the person has important new dimensions for persons suffering from grave and irremediable medical conditions. The new matrix of law and fact on which the Court relied included principles of fundamental justice under section 7 of the Charter and an uptick in public support for physician-assisted suicide, as well as support from the medical profession. According to new evidence from permissive jurisdictions, concerns about the potential for abuse that had clearly influenced the Court in the 1993 ruling do not appear to have been borne out. In striking down the prohibition in the *Criminal Code* on assisted suicide, the Court created a positive obligation on the federal government to design a new regime, with all of its attendant programs, costs, and institutional investments, thus allowing people to benefit in practice from the ruling.

Should we reverse all these protections, rights, and legal developments because of an abstract worry about too many rights and too much law? How will we decide a priori which rights should be brought before the courts and which should not? Which protections should we give up? And who will choose?

YES, BUT ARE THEY REAL RIGHTS?

Is it true that human rights no longer deal with real rights at all, but rather with watered-down or trivial versions of "real" rights? The most striking examples of these critiques have been directed at human rights commissions, whose officials are sometimes cast as officious bureaucrats trolling for fringe claims from "surgery-seeking transsexuals," say, or "unhygienic foreigners" who won't wash their hands, thus creating what critics see as a self-perpetuating cottage industry of dubious claims.[28]

But this argument depends on a fallacy. Confusing *where* the right is being claimed with the right itself can indeed make cases appear bizarre. For example, the sit-ins and protests at lunch counters by African Canadians in southern Ontario in the 1960s could be reframed as fighting for the "the right to have lunch." The famous case of Viola Desmond, a black woman who was thrown out of a Nova Scotia theatre in the 1940s, could be recast as a struggle for "the right to go to the movies."[29]

More often than not, when one takes a closer look at the seemingly weird cases, the "real" right is easy enough to discern and is neither novel nor trivial. One case that attracted scrutiny in Canada illustrates the point: a "handwashing claim" brought against the McDonald's fast food chain in British Columbia in 2007 by Beena Datt. An immigrant from Fiji, Datt had worked at McDonald's for twenty-three years. Over time, Datt developed a painful and debilitating skin allergy to the soap used at the workplace. The medical evidence illustrated that her hands had become "unusable." She ended up losing her job. Datt filed a human rights complaint and won her case.[30] Anti-commission activist Ezra Levant seized on the complaint to say that the decision was "crazy" and that restaurant industry workers would now be able to claim a "right" not to wash their hands.[31] *Maclean's* magazine, which published Levant's article, was on the front lines of the media assault against human rights commissions at the time because of the hate speech wars, and any article or commentary that was critical of these institutions appears to have been publishable in the mainstream media.

Levant's comments outraged Patricia Knipe, a journalist working in communications at the Manitoba Human Rights Commission. Knipe recalled reading an excerpt from Levant's book *Shakedown* about the *Datt* case in *Maclean's*. "The article got so many things wrong," she said. "I am a journalist and am protective of my profession. I was appalled that *Maclean's* would let people think that this was a real journalist writing about real news."[32] She disputed Levant's characterization of the decision as one that allowed employees to serve food without washing their hands. "In fact," she said,

> when you read the case, it is clear that the Tribunal was very cautious about public health and applauded McDonald's for its commitment to public health and hygiene. This element of the story was completely misrepresented. When you read the actual decision, you see the hard choices that both the employee and the employer had to make—what would happen to her employment, what would happen to an employee of twenty-three years?[33]

According to the BC Human Rights Tribunal, the crux of the case was that the employer should have made more efforts to find Datt another job and to investigate alternatives to the soap that had caused the skin condition. The BC tribunal did not conclude that workers preparing food should ignore hygiene standards. Rather, it took pains to point out that the employee's disability did not prevent her from undertaking other tasks or jobs and that Datt could have been accommodated without undue hardship to McDonald's.

Legal commentators recognized that the *Datt* case was not represented accurately in the media, and the tribunal's supposedly "crazy" analysis was subsequently cited with approval by the Supreme Court of British Columbia in 2011.[34] Why was the *Datt* case depicted as a "crazy" rights scenario? First, Datt was a soft target. The likelihood of an unemployed, immigrant fast food worker finding the wherewithal to mount a campaign to counter the views of an established media commentator was almost non-existent. As a neutral decision-maker, the tribunal would be unlikely to leap into the fray to correct misstatements. In short, it was not risky to count on the fact that there would be few challengers to the dyspeptic diatribes against BC's human rights tribunal, against Datt herself, or against the human rights system writ large. More importantly, the real devaluation of rights occurred because of the inaccurate notion that "a right not to wash your hands" if you worked in a restaurant now existed.

Another important area of so-called expansion or inflation of rights is immigration and refugee law. Preventing discrimination against non-citizens is not a complicated idea but it is a controversial one and, as a result of the migrant crisis in the Middle East, increasingly so. It was not clear in the early post-Charter days whether, or to what extent, refugee claimants in Canada had any human rights at all under the Charter. The Supreme Court of Canada's 1995 *Singh* case was important because it decided that persons physically present in Canada are entitled to life, liberty, and security of the person.[35] Critics were astonished that the word "everyone," as enshrined in the Charter, could actually be interpreted to mean "everyone."[36] The implications of *Singh* for diaspora communities, immigrants, and refugees, in providing an opportunity to share in the rights and wealth Canada offers, are significant.[37]

Barriers to inclusion in Canadian society have been dismantled one by one, and they are numerous: the lack of recognition of foreign credentials, exclusionary "Canadian experience" requirements, constraints on family reunification, limited paths to citizenship for temporary workers, and uneven access to social security protections and benefits. It would be easy to dismiss the outcomes as inflationary "new rights." The opposite is true. Establishing access to health care and social services adds value because such measures help new arrivals become active contributors in Canadian life. Sadly, legal challenges have often been necessary to make these basic services accessible.[38] Social justice is not justice at all when people are barred from exercising their rights or from seeking remedial action to address rights violations.

Family status is another new area of human rights law, introduced as a ground of non-discrimination in Ontario in 1982, twenty years after Ontario's first *Human Rights Code*. It was initially intended to prevent discrimination against people because they have children, and similar protections now exist in most of Canada. In 1989 the Supreme Court of Canada said that the unique role played by women was such that it would be unfair to impose all of the costs of pregnancy solely on women who choose to work outside the home.[39] Between 1993 and 1995, "family status" formed the basis of only about 3 percent of human rights claims in Ontario. In 2013–14, it accounted for 12 percent of claims.[40]

In 2006, in an important case, the Canadian Human Rights Tribunal ruled that the employer, Canadian National Railway (CN), must be more flexible in scheduling the shifts of an employee whose child had special needs.[41] CN had taken three months to accommodate the needs of Ms. Hoyt, who had experienced complications during her pregnancy. When Hoyt moved to a new position after this delay, CN refused to accommodate her child care needs, offering only unpaid leave and making no effort to reschedule her shifts when she could not arrange child care. CN was found in breach of its duty to accommodate the employee based on family status.

The scope of the protection offered by "family status" has continued to expand because of a more fluid and inclusive notion of "family." There are more single parents, more families with two working parents, more blended families, and more families caring for older parents. Employment standards law allows parents to take some form of caregiving leave, but this is not the same thing as obliging employers to adjust their workplace schedules, job descriptions, or shifts to accommodate employees. Canada already has extensive human rights protections on the grounds of sex, but caregiving and its relationship to family status is a newer frontier, one that is expanding for a range of policy reasons that reflect our evolving definitions of family as well as imposing part of the burden of caring for dependents on employers.

EQUALITY RIGHTS VERSUS OTHER RIGHTS

Implicit in the critique that equality rights are a threat to "real rights" is the assertion that equality rights and social and economic rights are subordinate or inferior to, for instance, freedom of speech or the right to vote.[42] As discussed earlier, a related concern is that so-called positive rights are threatening (at least in Canada) to swamp negative rights, which entail a narrower and less interventionist approach by the courts. But it is now well established that human rights are interdependent and that very few can be meaningfully articulated or practically implemented, let alone enforced, in isolation. The Supreme Court of Canada has rejected the idea that there is a hierarchy of importance among human rights.[43]

Embedded in the concern about equality rights and their connection to so-called positive rights is the concern that courts will impose policies or programs that are better left to legislators. Housing rights is a good example. The right to adequate housing is a fundamental human right enshrined in international law: the International Covenant on Economic, Social and Cultural Rights requires that every state provide an adequate level of housing.[44] The great jurist Albie Sachs was a member of the South African Constitutional Court that rendered a decision in *Government of South Africa v. Grootboom et al.*, which recognized that South Africa had an obligation to provide decent housing for the many poor people who were living in informal and inadequate housing arrangements after apartheid ended.[45] A generous and expansive interpretation of South Africa's constitution, including a recognition of the fundamental obligation to help the poorest and most vulnerable, was a signal achievement. Although South Africa is still a developing country with enormous wealth disparities, it performs better than most sub-Saharan African states when it comes to housing.[46] The *Grootboom* case is an important part of that story.

In Canada, public recognition of housing rights lags far behind our own human rights commissions and tribunals, which for decades have provided at least partial protection of the right to housing. However, outside the purview of human rights legislation, adequate housing is viewed as an aspiration best left to legislatures, not as a genuine and justiciable right. An editorial on homelessness published in the *Globe and Mail* in 2010 declared that only elected legislators, not unelected judges, have the expertise to establish social programs and choose between competing interests. The editorial warned that allowing the courts to deal with housing issues (including the fight against homelessness) could lead to "a myriad of social problems" and battles for scarce resources.[47]

Decisions about how to allocate scarce resources do belong with legislatures, at least in the first instance. But it should not be necessary to point out that we also have a *Charter of Rights and Freedoms* as well as human rights laws that impose a legal framework to which government decisions are subject. Notwithstanding suggestions that the courts have run amok and judges are legislating from the bench, a review of Supreme Court decisions shows that claims of judicial activism, in the sense of inappropriate incursions into legislative powers, are highly suspect.[48]

Judicial progress on housing rights has been slow. In June 2015 the Supreme Court of Canada dismissed an application for leave in *Tanudjaja, et al. v. Attorney General of Canada, et al.*[49] There had been high hopes that this Ontario case would open the doors to wider recognition of equality rights by the courts under section 15 of the Charter. It was argued that the insecurity caused by inadequate housing gave rise to a prima facie violation of section 7 of the Charter, which protects the right to life, liberty, and security of the person. At first instance, the court had dismissed the *Tanud-jaja* application on a preliminary basis because the case did not disclose a viable cause of action and there was no reasonable prospect of success. The Court of Appeal for Ontario upheld the dismissal.[50]

However, in the 2015 decision *Abbotsford (City) v. Shantz*, the Supreme Court of British Columbia struck down bylaws aimed at evicting homeless populations.[51] The case bore some resemblance to the South African *Grootboom* case in that it addressed the rights of precariously housed or homeless people evicted from the only shelter available to them. Although the court in *Abbotsford* did not create a right to adequate housing, it did decide that the eviction notices were grossly disproportionate and that the bylaws violated the principles of fundamental justice inherent in section 7 of the Charter.

Litigants have sometimes had to work around the courts' limited interpretations of sections 7 and 15 of the Charter by relying on ordinary statutes to bootstrap their claims into arguments for substantive rights. The 2007 *VIA Rail* case, for example, involved a complaint made by the Council of Canadians with Disabilities to the Canadian Transportation Agency.[52] The issue was the lack of accessibility to the VIA Rail Renaissance cars for wheelchair users. However, for precisely the reasons suggested earlier, the council decided not to risk the outcome by relying on the court's heretofore limited application of equality rights inherent in section 15 of the Charter; instead it focused (successfully) on the provisions of the *Canadian Transportation Act*.

Dominique Clément objects to the right of disabled children to receive an education and opposes the resort to human rights legislation, arguing that litigation is inappropriate.[53] His objection is a response to the 2012 Supreme Court case *Moore v. British Columbia*. Jeffrey Moore's parents sought intensive remedial instruction for Jeffrey because of his severe dyslexia.[54] Without remedial instruction, Jeffrey would have been unable to read or write at a functional level. Following government cutbacks, the only available public diagnostic centre had been closed, thus ending access to public programs in British Columbia for people with severe learning disabilities. Jeffrey could have obtained intensive and effective remedial instruction only at a private school. Jeffrey's father filed a complaint with the BC Human Rights Tribunal on behalf of his son.

Evidence presented before the tribunal showed that intensive supports are necessary for children with severe learning disabilities and that early intervention is important. In a lengthy decision, tribunal chair Heather MacNaughton ruled that both the Ministry of Education and the school district were liable for costs related to discrimination against Moore, not only for tuition at a private school and remedial instruction, but also for implementing a broad range of remedial measures designed to ensure the availability of early intervention programs.[55] The case went up on review to the Supreme Court of British Columbia, where the reviewing judge decided there had been no discrimination. The Court of Appeal also dismissed the appeal. But the Supreme Court of Canada restored the tribunal's order against the school district. The school district had argued that its financial situation left it no choice but to terminate the special learning programs and to close the diagnostic centre, but the Court decided that the school district had failed to consider alternatives for special needs students. Justice Abella wrote the Supreme Court's unanimous decision and articulated a powerful argument for state responsibility to educate all children, based on provincial education legislation:

> The reason all children are entitled to an education is because a healthy democracy and economy require their educated contribution. Adequate special education, therefore, is not a dispensable luxury. For those with severe learning disabilities, it is the ramp that provides access to the statutory commitment to education made to *all* children in British Columbia.[56]

It is important to point out that the decision did not impose a particular program on the school district, but it did impose a positive obligation on the school district to consider alternatives when children with disabilities effectively lose access to public education.

Furthermore, in cases like this, parents always try administrative options and negotiations before embarking on the arduous and expensive route of litigation.

INTERNATIONAL HUMAN RIGHTS LAW

Since the 1970s, Canada has ratified many treaties generically referred to as human rights instruments. Many of the rights protected in recent human rights instruments might be considered "new." As discussed earlier, the 1990 CRC, which adapted rights and principles from other human rights instruments for children, ensures that states interpret rights in accordance with the fundamental principle of children's best interests. The prohibition against incarcerating children with adult offenders in the prison population is an example. The detention of certain immigrants and refugee claimants pending determination of their claims sometimes results in the incarceration of children in adult facilities, a clear violation of international law.[57] Critics might see the CRC as conferring a "new right" by prohibiting the incarceration of children with adult populations. In fact, it reflects a long-standing and foundational requirement that states act in the best interests of children, and the right to be separated from the adult population is an adaptation of that general principle to a specific circumstance.

Other "new" rights include the prohibition against enforced disappearances, one of the more recent international norms set out in a human rights convention developed in 2010.[58] It may be a "new right," but it is designed to combat a crime against humanity. Activists and lawyers in countries like Sri Lanka, among many others, have discovered that without specific norms to deal with disappearances, state lawyers have been able to argue successfully that no human rights violation took place because no one could produce a body.

Objections to rights expansionism and inflation presume that certain rights (referred to sometimes, and in error, as core rights) are inherently more important than others or that a multiplicity of the "wrong" kind of rights somehow detracts from the "real" ones. To start with, there is a definitional problem here: international human rights law recognizes that "core rights" include not only the fundamental freedoms, such as freedom of expression and religion, but also economic and social rights, such as the right to housing and education.[59] More importantly, international law rejects "hierarchies" of rights (as does Canadian law) and has done so for more than two decades.[60] It is regressive to respond to the long-standing and organic relationship between international human rights law and Canada's Charter by simply dismissing the relevance of the former to the latter. International human rights law was an important inspiration for Canada's Charter, and Canada is legally obligated to respect, protect, and fulfill the international human rights it has adhered to or ratified as a matter of law—a point the Supreme Court of Canada has made on multiple occasions.

It is important, however, to understand that even while rejecting rights hierarchies, decision-makers are still capable of reconciling rights in a given context. A rejection of rights hierarchies does, however, mean that one type of right cannot make a priori and de jure claim to trump another. The two groups of rights (civil and political, and economic, social, and cultural) emerged in international law at the same time. Critics who are wedded to a classic civil libertarian model of post–Cold War and pre-Charter rights have been reluctant to place civil liberties under the rubric of equality rights, or to recognize rights that operate in a more progressive context, such as economic and social rights. "There is something generational about the idea that the 'great freedoms' are not about equality, and this may be linked to the Cold War," says Emeritus Law Professor Ken Norman. "Look what happened to Franklin Roosevelt's second bill of rights—the Cold War killed it dead. People who think that economic and social rights are bolshie sorts of socialism are out there, but that generation is slowly but surely leaving."[61]

It is worth recalling that economic and social rights are among the oldest human rights protections in Canada: education, housing, employment, and social services are enshrined in human rights and non-discrimination statutes dating back to the 1960s. In fact, ten out of fourteen human rights jurisdictions in Canada also prohibit discrimination based on social condition, social origin, and/or source of income, although the scope of protection varies.[62] Canada ratified the International Covenant on Economic, Social and Cultural Rights more than thirty years ago, at the same time it confirmed the International Covenant on Civil and Political Rights. Human rights commissions and tribunals have been dealing with complaints with respect to economic and social issues for years, with little fanfare and without the sky falling in.

CONCLUSION

Duly elected Canadian legislatures have enacted human rights laws in response to evolving social mores, constitutional developments, and international human rights law. Even within the confines of familiar and existing grounds like disability, race, and sex, which still account for the vast majority of complaints, the way in which human rights cases are described, understood, and litigated has changed dramatically over the years. The same is true for civil, political, and a host of other rights.

Far from being "inflationary," the human rights evolution has taken place in direct response to new human problems and has sought to provide meaningful solutions that add value to human life and societies. This is ongoing, iterative work. The real crisis, if there is one, is that rights are being devaluated as a result of attempts to artificially limit or freeze them in time. When responding to critiques about too many rights, taking the longer view brings into focus the richness of the rights evolution and the inherent simplicity and unity of claims grounded in equality, freedom, and human dignity. To ask which rights we should remove, and from whom we might remove them, is to invite the blustery non-answer the Emperor offered Mozart: "Well. There it is."

Surely we can do better.

Notes

This chapter draws in part from *Speaking Out on Human Rights: Debating Canada's Human Rights System* (Montreal and Kingston: McGill–Queen's University Press, 2014). Readers may also be interested in the debate I had with Dominique Clément on the topic of this chapter on the CBC Radio show "The 180 with Jim Brown," during which many of the themes addressed in this chapter were raised

("Are we asking for too many rights?" 4 June 2015). http://www.cbc.ca/radio/the180/rethinking-the-canada-first-nations-relationship-hold-the-applause-and-carry-on-limits-1.3098923/debate-are-we-asking-for-too-many-rights-1.3100149 [CBC Radio].

1 See Andrew Clapham, *Human Rights: A Very Short Introduction* (Oxford: Oxford University Press, 2007).
2 Eliadis, *Speaking Out*, note 1, Chapter 3.
3 See, in particular, Eric A. Posner, *The Twilight of Human Rights Law* (New York: Oxford University Press, 2014).
4 Eliadis, *Speaking Out*, note 1, Table 3.1 at 11.
5 See, for example, "National Post View: Too many rights make wrong," *National Post*, 3 June 2015), http://news.nationalpost.com/full-comment/national-post-view-too-many-rights-make-wrong.
6 *Reference re Same-Sex Marriage*, [2004] 3 S.C.R. 698, 2004 SCC 79 at para. 33, in reference to the division of powers between sections 91 and 92 of the *Constitution Act*, 1982.
7 *Singh v. Minister of Employment and Immigration*, [1985] 1 SCR 177.
8 *CN v. Canada (Canadian Human Rights Commission)*, [1987] 1 SCR 1114.
9 *Janzen v. Platy Enterprises Ltd*, [1989] 1 SCR 1252.
10 *Central Alberta Dairy Pool v. Alberta (Human Rights Commission)*, [1990]. In the school context, see *Multani v. Commission scolaire Marguerite-Bourgeoys*, [2006] 1 SCR 256.
11 *Moore v. British Columbia (Education)*, 2012 SCC 61.
12 *Eldridge v. British Columbia (Attorney General)*, [1997] 3 S.C.R. 624.
13 *Vriend v. Alberta*, [1998] 1 SCR 493.
14 *Carter v. Canada (Attorney General)*, 2015 SCC 5.
15 I have adapted the important and influential idea of human flourishing developed in the context of human rights and international law by Martti Koskenniemi, "The Politics of International Law" 1(4) European J. of Internal Law (1990) 4.
16 *International Covenant on Civil and Political Rights*, 19 December 1966, 999 UNTS 171, Can TS 1976 No 47, 6 ILM 368 (entered into force 23 March 1976, accession by Canada 19 May 1976) [ICCPR].
17 *Convention on the Rights of the Child*, 20 November 1989, 1577 UNTS 3, 28 ILM 1456 (entered into force 2 September 1990, ratification by Canada 13 December 1991).
18 *International Convention on the Protection of the Rights of All Migrant Workers and Members of their Families*, 18 December 1990, 2220 UNTS 3 (entered into force 1 July 2003).
19 *Convention on the Elimination of All Forms of Discrimination against Women*, 18 December 1979, 1249 UNTS 13, Can TS 1982 No 31, 19 ILM 33 (entered into force 3 September 1981, ratification by Canada 10 December 1981).
20 Report of the Special Rapporteur on the promotion and protection of the right to freedom of opinion and expression, Frank La Rue, UNGA 17th Session. A/HRC/17/27, 16 May 2011.

21   Interview, David Baker, in Eliadis, *Speaking Out.*
22   See Bill C-21, *An Act to Amend the Canadian Human Rights Act,* 2nd Sess., 39th Parl., 2008 (assented to 18 June 2008), SC 2008, c 30. The repeal took effect in 2011 after a three-year transitional period.
23   *Janzen v. Platy Enterprises Ltd,* [1989] 1 SCR 1252.
24   *Friedmann v. MacGarvie,* 2012 BCCA 445.
25   Eliadis, *Speaking Out,* note 14.
26   *Carter v. Canada (Attorney General),* 2015 SCC 5.
27   See *Rodriguez v. British Columbia (Attorney General),* [1993] 3 SCR 519.
28   See, for example, Margaret Wente, "Human Rights Commissions—a Day at the Theatre of the Absurd," *Globe and Mail* (16 February 2008), A19; Margaret Wente, "The Explosive Rethinking of Sex Reassignment," *Globe and Mail,* 25 August 2007, A19; Ezra Levant, "Enough's enough—exclusive excerpt: How McDonald's hand-washing policy was overruled, *Maclean's,* 2 April 2009, http://www.macleans.ca/news/canada/enoughs-enough.
29   *His Majesty the King v. Viola Irene Desmond,* Halifax, Public Archives of Nova Scotia (RG 39, "C" Halifax, v. 937, Supreme Court of Nova Scotia, No. 13347; *The King v. Desmond* (1947), 20 Maritime Provinces Reports 297 (Nova Scotia Supreme Court). Cited in Constance Backhouse, "The Historical Construction of Racial Identity and Implications for Reconciliation," report commissioned by the Department of Canadian Heritage for the Ethnocultural, Racial, Religious and Linguistic Diversity of Identity Seminar (2001) at 17. *Metropolis,* http://canada.metropolis.net/events/ethnocultural/publications/historical.pdf.
30   *Datt v. McDonald's Restaurants (No. 3),* 2007 BCHRT 324.
31   Levant, "Enough's Enough."
32   Interview of Patricia Knipe, in *Speaking Out,* note 1.
33   Ibid.
34   See Ron Ellis, *Unjust by Design: Canada's Administrative Justice System* (Vancouver: UBC Press, 2013) at 82, discussing *Emergency Health Services Commission v. Cassidy,* 2011 BCSC 1003 (CanLII).
35   *Singh v Canada (Minister of Employment and Immigration),* [1985] 1 SCR 177.
36   Madam Justice Bertha Wilson, speaking for three justices out of the six in the decision, said that Section 7 of the *Charter* is guaranteed not only for Canadian citizens but for "every human being who is physically present in Canada and by virtue of such presence amenable to Canadian law," ibid. at 201–2.
37   Jeffrey Simpson comments on the *Singh* case and blames it on the cost of refugee adjudication. See "Blame the refugee system," *Globe and Mail,* 14 July 2009, http://www.theglobeandmail.com/news/opinions/blame-the-refugee-system/article1218134. Such comments and concerns about Canada's supposed softness regarding fraudulent refugees have circulated for years. See, for example, "Debating the Numbers" and "Is Canada a Soft Touch?" *Maclean's,* 7 November 1994, 22, 28.
38   See, notably, *Canadian Doctors for Refugee Care v. Attorney General of Canada and Minister of Citizenship and Immigration,* 2014 FC 651.
39   *Brooks v Canada Safeway Ltd.,* [1989] 1 SCR 1219 at 1244.

40 Ontario Human Rights Commission, *Annual Report 1993–1994 and 1994–1995* (Toronto: Government of Ontario, 1996); *Ontario Human Rights Tribunal Statistics 2013–2014* (Toronto: Social Justice Tribunals of Ontario, 2015). As at November 2016, the 2013–14 annual report has not been posted by the HRTO.

41 *Hoyt v Canadian National Railway*, [2006] CHRT No. 33 (CHRT). See also *Johnstone v Canada (AG)*, [2007] FCJ No. 43 aff'd [2008] FCJ No. 47 (CA).

42 In a 1999 interview with Terry O'Neill of the *BC Report* newsmagazine, Stephen Harper called human rights commissions, which protect a hybrid of equality rights, and economic, social, and cultural rights in Canada, an "attack on fundamental freedoms and the basic existence of a democratic society" (excerpted in *Maclean's*, "Harper must act now to protect free speech," 20 September 2009). The refrain was taken up multiple times by conservative commentators, litigants, and civil society organizations, including the Canadian Constitution Foundation and the Justice Centre for Constitutional Freedoms. See also Tom Flanagan, "Time to right some wrongs," *Globe and Mail*, 19 May 2009.

43 See, for example, *Gosselin (Tutor of) v. Quebec (Attorney General)*, [2005] 1 SCR 238.

44 *International Covenant on Economic, Social and Cultural Rights*, Article 11 (Canada acceded to the Covenant in 1976).

45 *Government of South Africa v. Grootboom et al.* (2000) CCT 11/00.

46 Susan Randolph, Sakiko Fukudo-Parr, and Terra Lawson-Remer, *Economic and Social Rights Fulfillment Index: Country Scores and Rankings*, Economic Rights Working Paper Series, Working Paper no. 11 (Connecticut: Human Rights Institute, University of Connecticut, 2009), Table 5.

47 "This Is Not the Way Home" [Editorial], *Globe and Mail*, 27 May 2010, A14. The editorial was a response to a Charter challenge to homelessness filed on 26 April 2010.

48 Sujit Choudhry and Claire E. Hunter, "Measuring Judicial Activism on the Supreme Court of Canada: A Comment on *Newfoundland (Treasury Board) v. NAPE*," (2003) 48 McGill LJ 525.

49 Application for leave dismissed. *Jennifer Tanudjaja, et al. v. Attorney General of Canada, et al.* 2015-06-25 Case no. 36283.

50 *Tanudjaja v. Canada (Attorney General)*, 2014 ONCA 852.

51 2015 BCSC 1909.

52 *Council of Canadians with Disabilities v. VIA Rail Canada Inc.*, [2007] 1 SCR 650. See also David Baker and Sarah Godwin, "All Aboard! The Supreme Court of Canada Confirms That Canadians with Disabilities Have Substantive Equality Rights," (2008) 39 Sask L Rev 41.

53 CBC Radio, 2015, *supra* note 1.

54 *Moore v. British Columbia (Education)*, 2012 SCC 61.

55 *Moore v. B.C. (Ministry of Education) and School District No. 44*, 2005 BCHRT 580, at para. 612.

56 Ibid. at para. 5.

57 See the interesting discussion in Stephanie J. Silverman, "In the Wake of Irregular Arrivals: Changes to the Canadian Immigration Detention System," 30 Canada's J on Refugees no. 2, 2014, 27.

58 *International Convention for the Protection of All Persons from Enforced Disappearance*, 23 December 2010, UNTS, vol. 2716, 3, Doc. A/61/448.

59 See the list of "core rights" at OHCHR http://www.ohchr.org/EN/Profes sionalInterest/Pages/CoreInstruments.aspx.

60 United Nations, *Vienna Declaration and Programme of Action*, GA June 1993, World Conference on Human Rights, A/CONF 157/23 (1003), UNHCHR, http://www.unhchr.ch/huridocda/huridoca.nsf/(symbol)/a. conf.157.23.en.

61 Interview of Ken Norman, in Eliadis, *Speaking Out*.

62 Grounds such as social condition or social origin and protections based on receipt of public assistance or source of income are found in ten out of fourteen human rights systems in Canada.

Liberalism, Social Democracy, and Human Rights

Rhoda E. Howard-Hassmann

SOCIAL JUSTICE VS. HUMAN RIGHTS

Dominique Clément's key argument is that framing all perceived social injustices in Canada as human rights violations undermines civic debate. Social justice, he argues, is a wider and more debatable concept than human rights. To frame all aspects of social justice as human rights violations is to invite all-or-nothing judicial solutions to matters that should be the subject of public policy, decided not by judges but by politicians, who have the leeway to devise compromise solutions to complex problems. It is also to permit judges or human rights tribunals to make decisions about citizens' rights without consideration of distributional priorities, as if there are no resource constraints that ought to be considered.

I have some sympathy with Clément's concerns about judicial solutions to complex social problems, but he undermines his case by positing several contradictory definitions of what social justice means. He maintains that "social justice is the pursuit of equality," but it is not clear what he means by equality. If he means political or legal equality, these are already covered by the universal and non-discriminatory principles of Canadian and international human rights law. If he means material equality, then this is a very limited definition. Moreover, immediately following his claim that social justice means the pursuit of equality, Clément goes on to argue that "social justice refers to those conditions that enable individuals to pursue their vision of the good life. Illiteracy, poverty, lack

121

of education or health care, and unemployment are violations of social justice because they restrict individuals' capability to pursue their desires." Yet the good life and equality are not synonymous. Depending on their circumstances, individuals seeking the good life might put more stress on freedom than on equality. Even if material equality is the goal, there must be some consideration of how much equality or inequality is necessary in a society to promote the good life for all.

These disparate definitions of social justice not only undermine Clément's argument but also point to its deficiency: he does not provide a clear conceptual distinction between social justice and human rights. In and of itself, the actual enjoyment of human rights is a significant aspect of the good life. If I can go to bed at night without worrying that the police will raid me during my sleep because of my political beliefs, if I know that I cannot be denied housing because of my sexual orientation, or if I know that I am eligible for certain jobs despite my ethnicity, then that is part of the good life I lead. Under international human rights law, moreover, many of the goals of the good life that Clément mentions are already minimum standards. The *International Covenant on Economic, Social and Cultural Rights* (ICESCR), which Canada ratified in 1976, protects the rights to food, health care, and education. Numerous comments on these rights from such entities as the United Nations Committee on Economic, Social and Cultural Rights further elaborate exactly what those minimum standards are, as in its 1999 General Comment No. 12 on the right to food.[1] Undernourishment, lack of health care, and lack of education are not simply social injustices: they are violations of international human rights law as it now stands, and as Canada agreed forty years ago.

Clément is on safer ground in pointing out that there should be room in Canada for public policy decisions about what constitutes the good life, rather than so many decisions' being non-negotiable matters of law. He argues, "It has become common to frame issues of social justice as human rights. But social justice and human rights are not the same thing. If social justice is a dialogue around grievances against the state and society, then human rights are those core principles that make the dialogue possible." Even though many of the problems of social injustice to which Clément refers are already covered by international human rights law, that law in and of itself cannot provide the resources necessary to remedy material inequalities or complete denial even of the minimum necessary standards, as is the case for Canada's Indigenous peoples.[2] International human rights law is soft—that is, unenforceable. The most that entities such as the United Nations Human Rights Committee, which issues commentaries on governments' reports on human rights, can do is make suggestions for reform or possibly shame governments into reforming.

This is not necessarily a bad thing. When judges or human rights tribunals issue their judgments, they may or may not consider resource scarcity or competing claims on those resources. As Clément rightly points out, politicians do have to consider such problems. Public payment for one person's very expensive medications, for example, can mean that other people don't get surgery or a hospital bed—an enormous problem, given Canada's aging population. Clément maintains that human rights are a discourse of absolutes. In such a discourse, there is little room for pragmatism, and this makes all disagreements matters of law, not of negotiable policy, with deadlocked conflicts as the result. In her commentary, Pearl Eliadis argues that this is not so; she shows that Canadian courts do suggest compromises and do take into account conflicting priorities and resource constraints. Nevertheless, it is the judges themselves who decide whether they should take resource scarcity into account, and they can ignore this problem if they rule that the law so requires.

Clément also argues that remediation of inequality should not be a human rights matter. In fact, under international law it is not; international law sets minimum standards but does not prohibit inequality or suggest its maximum permissible degree. I agree with Clément that the actual rate of permissible inequality in a society should be a matter for public debate. Some inequality, economists have found, is necessary to a successful strategy for national economic well-being and growth. Without material incentives and without a surplus, individuals will not save and invest. But how much inequality should be permitted, and what minimum wages or tax levels should be, are matters for public debate. In this sense, international human rights law is naive. Statements of principle about rights to food, health care, and education may be useful reminders that minimum standards must be maintained, but they cannot guide economic policy or take into account competing priorities.

These practical problems do not mean, however, that there should not be economic human rights. Clément rejects the idea of human rights to health care, housing, adequate food, and freedom from hunger, yet these rights are crucial to the dialogue on social justice that he favours. As both Nathalie Des Rosiers and Gert Verschraegen also note in their commentaries, an educated person is more able to participate in discussions about public policy constraints than an uneducated one; a person adequately fed and housed, and whose health is adequately protected, is more likely to participate than one who is undernourished, is homeless, or suffers from ill health. If a democracy is to be one of all citizens, not just of the prosperous few, then all citizens' economic human rights warrant attention. This is why the international human rights literature consistently emphasizes the interdependence and indivisibility of human rights. It is not only that without civil and political rights people cannot expect to have their economic human rights fulfilled: it is also that, without economic human rights, enjoyment of civil and political rights to political participation is honoured more in the breach than in actual practice.

CORE RIGHTS

Having posited several definitions of social justice, Clément argues that a narrow set of human rights can be differentiated easily from the wider issue of social justice. He argues that Canadians should focus on what he calls core rights and eschew attempts by social movements or other actors to define all cries for social justice as calls for new human rights. He limits his core rights to those he identifies in his historical analysis as having always been integral to rights talk. His list includes freedom of religion, association, assembly, press, and speech; equal treatment; and due process.

Clément does not provide his readers with criteria to distinguish, in 2018, what he might consider marginal or frivolous claims for human rights from legitimate claims. The reader is left to infer from his numerous examples what he considers legitimate. Nor is it clear that a proliferation of human rights claims has the potential to make human rights a "debased rhetoric." There is much discussion in the media and among private citizens whenever new rights claims are proposed, such as the right of a child with disabilities to special education or the right of a transgendered individual to state-supported sex reassignment surgery. But discussions like these are part of healthy democratic debate: it does not follow that such human rights claims are contributing to a "debased rhetoric."

Clément's list of core rights is based on his reading of Canadian history. Yet his own evidence shows how much historical contestation there has been over those rights. Any consensus about what ought to be core rights, if it exists at all, evolved over time and was subject to much backtracking, as in the overriding even of the basic liberal democratic right to habeas corpus during the 1970 October Crisis in Quebec, sparked by terrorist actions including the kidnapping of the British Trade Commissioner in that province and the cold-blooded murder of a provincial cabinet minister, Pierre Laporte. Consensus on liberal democracy in the nineteenth and twentieth centuries emerged from political and social action; similarly, today's social and political movements are involved in creating what may become a new consensus on economic human rights—including the rights to food, housing, education, and health care—in the twenty-first century.

One could, nevertheless, make a strong case for Clément's list of what ought to be human rights, arguing that they are strategically prior to the economic rights now considered in the international literature to be as important as civil and political rights. No rights are safe if citizens cannot express their opinions about state actions or bring their dissatisfaction about denial of rights to the attention of the state via the press or public demonstrations. Without such rights, they are at the mercy of the decisions of states, which can just as easily withhold provision of such basic economic human rights as food, housing, health care, and education as provide them.[3]

Attempts to specify lists of core rights are always fraught with danger. For example, some might argue that such lists should be based on empirically verifiable human needs, the assumption being that biological needs are always more important than others. One might assume, on the face of it, that individuals will trade off freedoms for material security—for example, freedom of religion for food. But we know that is not the case, as the many refugees from the Islamic State (IS) remind us: these Yazidi or Christian or Shi'a refugees are unwilling to trade their religious freedom for a materially secure life under IS. Wisely, Clément posits no theory of human nature to buttress his list of core rights; he simply states that these are the rights that have evolved alongside Canada's liberal democracy. I agree that they are necessary for a liberal democracy, but I would go further and argue that only social democracies can be fully rights-protective states. A social democracy is a variant of liberal democracy that views the social provision of economic security as an inherent part of respect for the individual citizen. A social democratic state protects and fulfills economic human rights in an attempt to protect citizens against market forces and reduce inequality.[4]

From the point of view of international law, core human rights are much wider than Clément's interpretation and include the economic human rights necessary for full social democracy. In 1988 the political theorist Jack Donnelly and I reduced the large and unwieldy list of about sixty rights in the *International Bill of Human Rights* (the 1948 *Universal Declaration of Human Rights*, the 1976 *International Covenant on Civil and Political Rights*, and the ICESCR) to ten.[5] We did this for purposes of assessment, not to argue that our list was of core rights. We proposed ten rights, divided into four categories, that we argued could act as proxies for almost the entire list of sixty. These categories were survival rights (right to life, right to food, right to health care); membership rights (right to a family, right not to suffer discrimination); protection rights (habeas corpus, existence of an independent judiciary); and empowerment rights (right to an education, free press, freedom of association).

We did not propose this list to argue that these rights had priority over others; nevertheless, the categories we derived are worth examining. Protection rights follow squarely in the liberal tradition, focusing on the key rights of habeas corpus and an independent judiciary capable of guaranteeing the rule of law without state interference. Survival rights, however, go beyond the liberal tradition, as we define the right to life not only as protection against execution by the state but also as having enough to eat and having assistance in cases of ill health. Membership rights reflect not only the liberal tradition of formal legal and political equality (non-discrimination) but also the communitarian principle that human beings realize themselves—at least in part—in collective organizations such as the family. Finally, empowerment rights stem in part from the liberal tradition, which includes a free press and freedom of association, but also encompass the right to education, so that citizens can take an active part in political debate. Our categories did not, then, reflect a strictly liberal democratic approach to the way societies should be designed and preserved; we accepted liberal human rights as key but went beyond them to economic human rights, reflecting a social democratic approach.

Clément accepts the right to life but not the rights to health care or food, which he prefers to regard as public policy rather than justiciable matters, following Canada's liberal tradition. He argues that "claims for recognizing (and codifying in law) a human right ... to social services ... never had the type of popular appeal in the past as they do today," a statement that is somewhat surprising given Canadians' taken-for-granted assumptions over the past forty-five years about their rights to education and their fierce defence of the right to health care. In any event, despite Clément's reading of history, there was no consensus on liberal democratic rights in Canada until well into the twentieth century. Consensuses evolve through public discussion, activities of social movements, elite involvement, and indeed via the educative effects of national and international law.

Human rights are indeed historically contingent, as both Clément and Verschraegen note. Thus there is no reason that Canadians cannot come to a new consensus in which they decide that economic human rights are core rights. The principle that the state should ensure that citizens enjoy a right to subsistence was certainly not part of the evolving consensus, such as it was, on the meaning of human rights in nineteenth- and twentieth-century Canada, as Clément notes, stating that "there is no evidence that subsistence was integral to rights talk in Canada until recent history." This is a new, economic human right, one that reflects many Canadians' desire for a social democratic polity. But the fact that the right to subsistence is fairly recently integral to Canadian rights talk does not mean that a right to subsistence should not become a core right.

LIBERAL DEMOCRACY VS. SOCIAL DEMOCRACY

Todd Landman distinguishes between "thin" and "thick" democracy. The first, thinnest level of democracy is merely procedural: it allows contested elections with political participation. The next level is liberal and includes civil and political rights, the rule of law, and the right to own property. This is the type of liberal democracy that could be established by protecting Clément's list of core rights. Finally, the "thickest" type is social democracy, in which a state endeavours to protect economic human rights, including the right to food.[6]

Clément would confine the concept of human rights to those that foster liberal democracy, rather than also including those that foster social democracy. Yet there is no reason why Canadian history has to stop at 1982, when the *Charter of Rights and Freedoms* enshrined Clément's core rights. This is particularly so if, as Clément argues and I agree, human rights are indeed a social construction. If this is the case, it is difficult to object to social movements and individual actors who argue for new human rights.

Clément contends that "we should understand human rights as it is practised in social life" instead of taking a top-down approach. Elsewhere he says that human rights are a sociological phenomenon, not a legal one, claiming that "human rights are a product of human interaction, not legal reasoning." But in fact, we can discuss human rights as a "bottom-up" sociological phenomenon *and* as a "top-down" legal regime. Law does not simply impose rules and penalties; it often reflects public opinion as translated into law by legislators. Public opinion is in turn the consequence of human interaction, as when anti-poverty activists encounter malnourished Canadians at food banks. Those at the "bottom" often find it useful to know what the law at the "top" says, for they can use the law as a tool in their political advocacy work.

The "top-down" international legal regime that Clément objects to does contain what might be viewed as a social democratic agenda, but more and more Canadians want such a legal regime, one that enshrines social democratic principles. As Clément notes, all Canadians possess legal rights to health care and primary and secondary education. Eliadis suggests in her commentary, moreover, that the right to education is already recognized as a human right in Canada, just as it is in the international human rights regime, especially the ICESCR. I see no reason why social movements should not refer to Canadian ratifications of international human rights treaties to buttress their cases for enshrining all economic human rights in Canadian law.

At the moment, Canadians do not appear to have either a legal or a human right to adequate food and freedom from hunger, as guaranteed in Article 11, sections 1 and 2 of the ICESCR. Perhaps they *should* have such a human right. In 2011–12, 5.8 percent of Canadian households were judged to be moderately food insecure, in the sense that the quality and quantity of their food was compromised, while another 2.5 percent were severely insecure, in the sense that their food intake was reduced.[7] We should be appalled that in a rich country such as Canada, one household in forty is food insecure. Even more appalling is the extent of food insecurity among Canada's Indigenous peoples. In 2012, according to one study, 28.2 percent of Indigenous households were food insecure, as opposed to 12.6 percent of all households; even worse, 8.3 percent of Indigenous households were severely food insecure, as opposed to 2.6 percent of all households.[8]

Clément argues that poverty in and of itself is not a human rights issue, although it is a matter for social justice. He is correct as a matter of law: neither Canadian law nor international human rights law outlaws poverty. Yet poverty-stricken Canadians should not have to rely on charity (food banks, church food drives, donations of leftover food by restaurants, etc.) in order to have enough to eat. The rights to adequate food and freedom from hunger as defined in the ICESCR are minimal standards that should be achievable in Canada, a rich, developed country, regardless of distributional priorities. If it takes a case at the Supreme Court to oblige governments to devote more public resources to the right to food—perhaps through raising the minimum wage and providing higher welfare allowances—then that is what a social democratic state requires. Access to food was not part of the consensus on human rights in the nineteenth and twentieth centuries (assuming that such a consensus existed), nor is it yet part of the consensus in twenty-first-century Canada. But if human rights are historically contingent, then Canadian history has not stopped, and social movement actors are free to argue that there should be a human right to food. In so doing, they are also free to refer to international law.

As human rights are enshrined in law (international as well as Canadian) and accepted by citizenries, they become social facts, as Clément accepts; that is, they become widely accepted normative principles guiding citizens' expectations of both the state and one another. If human rights are a social construction, then there is no reason why Canadian human rights law cannot extend beyond the core human rights of liberal democracy, especially as practised in the nineteenth and twentieth centuries. There is no reason to cut off the notion of "core" rights at a certain point in Canadian history. From the nineteenth to the mid-twentieth centuries and beyond, core liberal rights were deeply contested in Canada: they did not reflect a consensus. As Clément notes, Canadians did not enjoy universal suffrage until 1960, when on-reserve Indigenous individuals attained the vote; indeed, core non-discrimination principles were not enshrined in Canadian law until 1985, when the non-discrimination clauses of the Charter came into force.

Law reflects social change, but it also leads and educates. Thus over the past thirty years a consensus has evolved in Canada regarding liberal democratic civil and political rights. Social change may yet result in a consensus on economic human rights in Canada—rights to food as well as to education and health care. In the international human rights regime, these are core rights; they are not marginal human rights contributing to what Clément views as a "cacophony" of rights claims. There is no reason to cut off human rights at liberal democracy, rather than proceeding to the more comprehensive rights culture that social democracy requires.

Clément is nevertheless correct to question whether the policies I call social democratic should be rooted completely in human rights law; perhaps they would be better attained through negotiation, compromise, and pragmatism, as long as they reflect a basic democratic commitment to the well-being of the citizenry. He is right to argue that practical questions of resource allocation are not best settled by judiciaries. But when it ratified the ICESCR forty years ago, Canada committed itself to minimum standards of economic human rights. Clément argues that poverty is a social condition, which it is—but so, at one time, was disregard of the political views of ordinary folk, and so was discrimination against blacks and women. That a social phenomenon is endemic and not easily remediable does not mean it is entirely impervious to, or outside the range of, human rights law.

Clément argues that "principles espoused under international law are to be applied by governments in ways that are consistent with our rights culture." But cultures are not immutable, and Canadian culture in 2018 is far from being locked into liberal democratic principles. Indeed, many Canadians consider care for the poor to be intrinsic to what ought to be their culture of human rights. I look forward to the time when Canadian social activists take the existence of severe food insecurity to the Supreme Court. It would be interesting to see whether the Supreme Court rules that it is discriminatory, in the case of Indigenous peoples, or even whether it violates our international human rights commitments.

Historical Contingency and Human Rights Pluralism

Gert Verschraegen

A s soon as an important social controversy or problem emerges in our society, it is never too long before we begin debating the issue in terms of rights—and in some cases, human rights. In his thoughtful and rich essay, Dominique Clément draws our attention to the problems associated with the increasingly frequent use of human rights language, as well as the social, political, and legal consequences. There are, he tells us, significant dangers of "human rights inflation." To the extent that human rights are presented as the solution to all societal problems, human rights language can lose some of its symbolic value and strength. In contrast to a time—not that long ago—when human rights were used solely to describe and denounce severe violations of individual freedom, they have become a dominant strategy for framing all sorts of personal and collective grievances, ranging from a lack of paid holidays to air pollution. This evolution has the potential to erode the value and legitimacy of what Clément calls "core rights," such as the right to bodily integrity and the right to free speech.

Clément's elaboration of these developments is striking. At some points in his text you sit up and take notice, as when he describes how Canadian human rights commissions have become battlefields for determining the legitimacy of cuts to social programs or even high fees for wideband access. One indeed wonders about the broad range of grievances that are nowadays addressed by applying the language of universal human rights. Not every question of social justice and economic inequality is a human rights issue. Although I agree with much of what Clément writes regarding this evolution, there are aspects of his text that I find problematic. In the spirit of a sympathetic but critical response, I offer a couple of observations and comments that place aspects of his diagnosis in a slightly different light. While Clément's essay is extensive and ranges across a vast field of discussion, I focus on three partly intertwined issues. First, I elaborate on the sociological-historical contours of the main diagnosis of "human rights inflation." Starting from the idea of the historical contingency of human rights, I discuss the great dynamism, flexibility, and diversity of human rights discourse. Second, taking into account this radical historicity of human rights, I raise the question of whether it is possible and useful to delineate "core rights" within the broad family of human rights. Third, I examine how human rights claims routinely emanate from everyday social and political life in modern societies, and consider how to filter this seemingly ever-increasing flood of claims.

HISTORICAL CONTINGENCY AND HUMAN RIGHTS PLURALITY

Instead of viewing human rights as immutable moral and legal principles, Clément stresses the historical contingency of rights. Yet, as I argue, he does not follow through on this. It is well known that the history of human rights is complex and uncertain and has proceeded through different historical stages. Throughout their development, very different human rights emerged to address a variety of specific problems such as the need to curtail state power, guarantee free speech, end slavery, protect the possibility of association, and ensure the availability of education to all. In this respect, the consecutive generations of human rights took shape around different concerns and issues. The classical civil rights, which crystallize around the inviolability, security, and religious freedom of the individual person, arose during a struggle against the politics of absolutism.

These rights were intended mainly to prevent the intrusion of the state into the private sphere. But the emergence of economic and social rights (as reflected, for example, in child labour legislation) was in response to societal problems caused by the delinking of the monetary economy from the broader society.[1] Cultural rights arose as a response to patterns of cultural domination. They aimed to guarantee, for instance, free and equal access to linguistic and cultural forms of communication, as well as traditional practices, in an age of global standardization (for what is the meaning of the right to speak a language of your choice if the language has died out?).

Today this plurality of human rights is well accepted. Although some philosophers have tried to offer a short list of rights—mostly in the context of a highly diversified international society[2]—most human rights scholars have accepted the inherent pluralism and openness of human rights. Furthermore, from a sociological point of view, this plurality is not accidental, but linked to the very structure of our societies. According to the German sociologist Niklas Luhmann, for instance, the differentiation of fundamental rights mirrors and underpins the differentiation of modern society into different, relatively autonomous social spheres such as the economy, politics, the arts, education, science, and so forth. The variety of basic rights symbolizes the freedom of each subject in these different spheres of society and protects the autonomy of each societal sphere. The fundamental right of ownership, for instance, ensures the autonomy and logic of the economic sphere against intrusions of various other functional logics, such as politics, religion, or the family. The existence of such a right makes it worthwhile to invest where one sees an economic opportunity because one knows in advance that the fruits of this investment will not be arbitrarily taken away by the state (or other powerful organizations). Similarly, the right to freedom of research motivates individual researchers and enables the autonomy of science as a social system by preventing religion (e.g., the religiously motivated refusal of scientific findings), the economy (industrial manipulation of research), and so forth from interfering with research findings.

Yet the historical contingency of human rights entails more

than inherent pluralism. It also implies a fundamental alterability of existing rights and the ever-present possibility that new rights will emerge. Because of their fundamentally abstract character, basic rights constantly need to be interpreted in the light of changing circumstances; they need to be spelled out in concrete terms for each particular case (see Eliadis's contribution in this volume). Fundamental rights can be violated in many different ways, often in ways that were not foreseen when these rights were first conceived. For instance, the right to privacy, which was conceived about 120 years ago, now has to be reframed in a media environment in which personal information flows seamlessly and can no longer be controlled.[3] If the definition of privacy is itself in flux, how are we to interpret the rights of private information-holders, and how should states or firms construe their responsibilities to preserve privacy? This process of rethinking and reframing rights is not simply a matter of legal reasoning and judges interpreting cases. It also entails reviewing our social commitments concerning "what is worth protecting and why, for and against whom, through which kinds of social and institutional agency, by what means, to what extent and through which processes."[4]

In short, my understanding of the historical contingency of human rights necessitates a constant process of revising existing rights and, if necessary, working out new rights and new rights-bearing subjects. It does *not* entail a more or less stable set of core rights, as Clément posits. Human rights are universal legal concepts that may facilitate negotiated compromises and the careful balancing of competing rights claims (e.g., the right to privacy versus the right to free speech); however, they do not presuppose any fixed set of core rights. As Forst, Gosepath, and Menke explain:

> Since 1945, the idea of human rights has, on the one hand, evolved into a globally shared point of reference for the justification and critique of political orders; on the other hand, however, almost everything about human rights has been increasingly contested. As the 1948 Universal Declaration of Human Rights already constituted a compromise between various

positions, traditions, and languages, whose deep disagreements it could hardly conceal, the history of human rights since then has been marked by two simultaneous but contradictory developments. While the list of human rights has been continually expanded, producing the illusion of an equally expanding and deepening consensus in what people like to refer to as the international community, the history of human rights since the Universal Declaration is a history of unresolved quarrels not only about what to include in the list of human rights and how to react to violations of such rights, but also about what a "human right" actually is."[5]

Although Clément acknowledges that "core rights are not uncontested," I think the notion of core rights presupposes more continuity around rights throughout history than genuinely exists. Ever since the adoption of the *Universal Declaration of Human Rights* (1948) there have been numerous conflicts over both the scope and the proper interpretation of those rights. The controversy between the Western and the Soviet blocs over the relative legal importance assigned to civil and political liberties on the one hand and socioeconomic rights on the other is only the most obvious of such conflicts, one that led to the adoption of competing conventions in 1966. Even at the level of individual rights, there is little room to presuppose consensus. After all, specific claims to a right are often met with opposing interpretations to that same right (just consider the long-standing contests over the reach of freedom secured by property rights). Pushing this line of thought even further, one could also say that human rights at their core amount to the "right to dissent."[6] This is because in a society founded on a consensus around a set of fundamental rights, there would be no need of them. The human rights question comes up only when there is dissent. They "enable people to coexist under real conditions of structural dissent ... In spaces of consensus (which are undoubtedly neither few in number nor restricted in scope) or under conditions that favour a rational consensus reached through discourse, human rights can be dispensed with."[7]

WHAT ARE "CORE" HUMAN RIGHTS?

As I have just pointed out, our current, long and differentiated list of human rights arose as a response to a variety of specific yet ever-changing societal problems (see also the other contributions in this volume). This historical contingency of human rights does not square easily with the idea of an essential set of rights. Clément nevertheless argues in his essay that on this long and ever-expanding list, a set of core rights—freedoms of religion, association, assembly, the press, and speech, as well as the right to equal treatment and due process—should be privileged. According to him, these are the rights that have been integral to rights talk throughout Canadian history. Although I do not think that all human rights should be held in equal value,[8] I am rather skeptical about the possibility of and need for a set of "core" human rights. I see several problems here. One is that the identification of a smaller set of "core" rights does not account for the variety of problems that human rights have to solve and for their function of upholding the highly differentiated structure of modern society. The second problem has to do with the well-known issue of the "indivisibility of human rights"—that is, the logical and functional interconnectedness of human rights. Since I've already addressed the first problem above, let me elaborate here on the second.

In his attempt to delineate a set of core rights, Clément builds on the traditional opposition between civil and political rights versus socio-economic rights. Civil and political rights are generally seen as rights that protect individuals against intrusion by the state, while socio-economic rights are rights to protection by the state against want or need. The former are seen as justiciable whereas the latter are supposed to be inspirational and impose less concrete duties on the state. Although the *Universal Declaration of Human Rights* did not distinguish separate categories or groups of rights, the distinction between these sets of rights was given an institutional grounding by the adoption of two covenants: the *International Covenant on Civil and Political Rights* (ICCPR), which lists primarily negative duties of restraint and includes rights that are enforceable through the courts; and the *International Covenant on Economic, Social and Cultural Rights* (ICESCR), which mainly gives rise to positive duties and recognizes rights that are monitored primarily through regular reporting requirements.[9]

This division of rights has long been connected to the political and ideological "Cold War" struggle between Western countries, above all the United States. Western countries alleged—and in part continue to maintain—that only the first generation of civil and political rights constituted "real" individual rights with corresponding legal entitlements against governments. Socialist states argued that the practical enjoyment of civil and political rights was dependent on the guarantee of a sufficient level of economic, social, and cultural rights.[10] With the end of the Cold War this politicized division of human rights gave way to an understanding that emphasizes the equality, interdependence, or "indivisibility" of different human rights.[11] What, precisely, does this "political compromise" entail? First, it means that no set of human rights can claim priority over other human rights, because the fulfillment of civil and political rights depends heavily on an effective enjoyment of economic, social, and economic rights, and vice versa. Most human rights scholars have now accepted that the rights protecting individual freedom and agency are inherently connected to equality-promoting socio-economic rights. This is easy to see, for instance, in regard to the right to education. Ignorance is a barrier to the realization of civil and political rights because uneducated people often do not know what rights they have and what they can do to use and defend them. Freedom of speech seems of little use to an illiterate person. Hence I do not think that the different categories of human rights can simply be untied, for there are logical and functional connections between them (see also the contributions of Eliadis and Howard-Hassmann in this volume). Without basic socio-economic entitlements for all, the enjoyment of civil and political rights cannot be guaranteed. "Equally problematically, those without resources will find it hard to access the legal system to redress breaches of their rights. This means that even the most fundamental rights, such as the right not to be detained without trial, or subjected to torture, may be less available to those without socio-economic means than others."[12] Furthermore, the same argument can be applied vice versa, in that economic and social rights will usually be better protected in countries with a high level of enjoyment of civil and political rights.

Second, contrary to the idea that freedom-protecting civil and political rights imply predominantly duties of restraint, while socio-economic rights entail mainly positive duties, human rights cannot very coherently be distinguished by the kinds of duties to which they give rise. If human rights are to be secured to all, it does not make sense to take seriously only those constraints that derive from state power and to ignore other constraints on the ability of individuals to exercise their rights. Such constraints can arise as much from poverty, poor health, and lack of education as from state tyranny and political intolerance. The right to life, for instance, does not merely impose an obligation on the state to refrain from infringing on the physical integrity of individuals; it also includes the right not to die from reasonably preventable or avoidable illnesses. This in turn gives rise to a range of positive duties on the state. This obviously means that civil and political rights are today interpreted in a much broader manner than originally perceived in human rights theory and jurisprudence. In addition to respecting civil and political rights by restraining from government interference, states have the additional obligation to secure these rights through a comprehensive set of positive measures.[13] It also means that the expectations placed on states regarding the protection of specific rights tend to flow towards areas that were previously not connected to those rights. Nowak writes that

> the obligation to respect the social right to health means, for example, that states shall not interfere with traditional health practices and shall respect the right of women to reproductive health. The obligation to fulfill requires states to build hospitals and primary care facilities, to train and employ sufficient numbers of doctors and nurses, to ensure the progressive reduction of infant mortality and to provide all people the highest attainable standard of physical and mental health. Finally, the

obligation to protect means, for example, that states should protect vulnerable groups, such as children, against practices by their parents and families that are detrimental to their health.[14]

Taking this idea of the "indivisibility of human rights" seriously hence leads to a certain "inflation" of claims made in the name of "human rights." At the very least, it gives rise to a more differentiated and complex set of duties imposed on the state and other actors, which can be held responsible for realizing respect for human rights. In this sense I concur with Clément's diagnosis of rights inflation. However, I do not think the remedy for this lies in a return to a set of "core" human rights. One of the main advantages of the doctrine of the indivisibility of human rights is that it has politically compromised the long-standing ideological division of rights by putting them on equal footing, thus also acknowledging the multiplicity and functional interconnectedness of human rights.[15] It does not seem particularly useful to backtrack on this political and conceptual evolution.

THE RISE OF HUMAN RIGHTS CLAIMS

But how then to conceive of the seemingly ever-increasing claims about justice and human rights that arise from individuals as well as communities and movements in civil society? And how to find ways of limiting this flood of claims? I do not aspire to have a final answer to these questions; rather, I want to emphasize some societal and cultural factors underlying the trend towards human rights inflation. I also want to consider the capacity of our political and legal institutions to filter these claims.

A first point I would like to stress is that the growing popularity of human rights language is not an isolated and insular evolution. It is inextricably linked to broader societal and cultural evolutions. To understand why human rights are increasingly being used as a language to frame all sorts of grievances, it is important to see how it is embedded in wider cultural belief systems or "collective imaginaries." Human rights are not just an abstract set of entitlements that are being understood and produced solely by professionals such as judges and lawyers. Rights claims "routinely emanate out of ordinary social life, often independent of direct influence from lawyers, judges, and state officials."[16] In recent decades, human rights have in effect become a dominant cultural frame for making sense of our changing identities in this world. Human rights offer "a language structure of words and shared understandings which agents appeal to when acting out their social lives."[17] They are a channel through which individuals can represent their rights and aspirations to themselves as well as to others. The language of human rights is attractive because it speaks to our individualism, enabling us to see ourselves as autonomous beings able to raise legal claims, yet it also connects us to a global "imagined community" that provides us with the minimum recognition of abstract humanity. When individuals or social movements refer to their human rights (as in "Lesbian Rights are Human Rights"), they call on these broader, symbolic resources of human rights, even when they do not actually want to use legal strategies.

As well, social movements and individuals have more strategic reasons for defining their problems in human rights terms. Reference to universal values "facilitates the international export of claims and allows social movements to frame demands in a way that does not emphasize particular interests."[18] Human rights appear to be compatible with a broad variety of political orientations. They are sufficiently broad in interpretive scope, inclusivity, flexibility, and cultural resonance to function as "a master frame" that facilitates the integration of multiple ideologies and moral systems.[19] At the same time, activists can use human rights to initiate political action and transform ordinary perceptions of what is just and unjust. Because human rights are supposed to have universal standing, they have critical purchase in relation to structures of injustice and suffering.

From this perspective, the proliferation of human rights claims is far from surprising. The advantages and the symbolic surplus of human rights make it appealing to mobilize this master frame. This is no cause for alarm, however. At least in the daily practice of law, the influence of rights claims seems rather limited. After all, specific claims of rights make it into court only if they get through the official legal procedures that assess and adjudicate the merits of competing claims. Even if a case is manufactured and financed by social movements or NGOs, the court will be obliged to settle cases between adversarial parties according to the rules and procedures of the legal system, which limits the possibilities of rights claiming to the terms of what is legally permissible. It can be argued that through this process, judges typically

> "kill" off far more than affirm visions of rights that bubble up from below, and that coordinated state "violence" necessarily enforces these narrow, select, traditionally bound constructions of rights on subjects. Law is words, but what makes words into law is the jurispathic violence that narrows the range of acceptable appropriations of rights talk in institutional practice and then systematically obscures or "forgets" the legal violence to both novel ideas and vulnerable bodies in the name of those circumscribed official norms.[20]

In this sense, the dangers of "human rights inflation" seem to be limited.

Notes

1   See Gert Verschraegen, 'Differentiation and Inclusion: A Neglected Socio-logical Approach to Fundamental Rights," in *Making Human Rights Intelligible: Towards a Sociology of Human Rights*, ed. Mikael Rask Madsen and Gert Verschraegen (Oxford: Hart, 2013).

2   For instance, Joshua Cohen, "Minimalism about Human Rights: The Most We Can Hope For?," *Journal of Political Philosophy* 12, no. 2 (2004): 190–213.

3   See Katayoun Baghai, "Privacy as a Human Right: A Sociological Theory," *Sociology* 46, no. 5 (2011): 951–65; Adam Thierer, "The Pursuit of Privacy in a World Where Information Control Is Failing," *Harvard Journal of Law & Public Policy* 36, no. 2 (2013): 409–56.

4   Sheila Jasanoff, "Introduction: Rewriting Life, Reframing Rights," in *Reframing Rights: Bioconstitutionalism in the Genetic Age*, ed. Sheila Jasanoff (Cambridge, MA: MIT Press, 2011).

5   Rainer Forst, Stefan Gosepath, and Christoph Menke, "Introduction," *Constellations* 20, no. 1 (2013): 5–6.

6   Wolfgang Welsch, "Gesellschaft ohne Meta-Erzählung?," in *Die Modernisierung moderner Gesellschaften. Verhandlungen des 25. Deutschen Soziologentages*, ed. Wolfgang Zapf (Frankfurt am Main and New York:

Campus, 1991), 174–84; Marcelo Neves, "The Symbolic Force of Human Rights," *Philosophy and Social Criticism* 33, no. 4 (2007): 411–44.

7   Neves, "The Symbolic Force of Human Rights," 420.

8   There is, in effect, substantial priority variation within human rights. For example, when the right to life conflicts with the right to privacy, the latter will generally be outweighed.

9   Sandra Fredman, *Human Rights Transformed: Positive Rights and Positive Duties* (Oxford: Oxford University Press, 2008), 66.

10 Manfred Nowak, "Indivisibility of Human Rights," in *The Essentials of Human Rights*, ed. Rhona K.M. Smith and Christien van den Anker (London: Routledge, 2005), 178–80.

11 This understanding has been officialized in paragraph 5 of the 1993 Vienna Declaration and Programme of Action, which reads as follows: "All human rights are universal, indivisible and interdependent and interrelated. The international community must treat human rights globally in a fair and equal manner, on the same footing, and with the same emphasis."

12 Fredman, *Human Rights Transformed*, 67.

13 Nowak, "Indivisibility of Human Rights," 179; Fredman, *Human Rights Transformed*.

14 Nowak, "Indivisibility of Human Rights," 180.

15 This change in human rights theory and in the broad evaluation of different categories of rights does not mean, however, that there is no hierarchy any more in human rights protection. In most countries, breaches of civil and political rights are considered more serious and are hence more likely to lead to remedial action.

16 Michael McCann, "The Unbearable Lightness of Rights: On Sociolegal Inquiry in the Global Era," *Law and Society Review* 48, no. 2 (2014): 245–73 at 248.

17 Darren O'Byrne, "On the Sociology of Human Rights: Theorising the Language-structure of Rights," *Sociology* 46, no. 5 (2012): 829–43 at 833.

18 Priscilla Claeys, "The Creation of New Rights by the Food Sovereignty Movement: The Challenge of Institutionalizing Subversion," *Sociology* 46, no. 5 (2012): 844–60 at 847.

19 Ibid., 847.

20 McCann, *The Unbearable Lightness of Rights*, 250.

Contributors

Dominique Clément

Dominique Clément is a Professor in the Department of Sociology at the University of Alberta and a member of the Royal Society of Canada (CNS). He is the author of *Canada's Rights Revolution*, *Equality Deferred*, and *Human Rights in Canada*. He is also the co-editor for *Alberta's Human Rights Story* and *Debating Dissent*. Clément has been a Visiting Scholar in Australia, China, and the United Kingdom. He has consulted for the Canadian Human Rights Commission and the Canadian Museum for Human Rights, and is currently on the Board of Directors for the Canadian Civil Liberties Association, the Centre for Constitutional Studies, and the Canadian Committee on Women's History. Clément manages an expansive website, HistoryOfRights.ca, which serves as a research and teaching portal on human rights in Canada.

Nathalie Des Rosiers

Nathalie Des Rosiers is a Member of the Provincial Parliament in Ontario for Ottawa–Vanier. She is the former general counsel for the Canadian Civil Liberties Association and Dean (Common Law) of the Faculty of Law at the University of Ottawa. She was previously Interim Vice-President Governance (2008–9) and Dean of the Civil Law Section at the University of Ottawa (2004–8), as well as President of the Law Commission of Canada (2000–4). She has been a member of the Environmental Appeal Board of Ontario and the Pay Equity Board of Ontario, a Commissioner of the Ontario Law Reform Commission, and a board member of the

Law Commission of Ontario. She also served as the President of the Federation of Social Sciences and Humanities, President of the Canadian Council of Law Deans, and President of the Canadian Association of Law Teachers and of the Association des juristes d'expression française de l'Ontario. She has received many honours, including the Order of Canada in 2013, the Order of Ontario in 2012, an Honorary Doctorate from the UCL (Université catholique de Louvain) in Belgium in 2012, an Honorary Doctorate from the Law Society of Upper Canada, the Medal from the Law Society of Upper Canada, the NUPGE Award, and the APEX Partnership Award, and was named one of Canada's twenty-five most influential lawyers in both 2011 and 2012.

Pearl Eliadis

Pearl Eliadis, B.C.L., LL.B., B.C.L. (Oxon.) is a human rights lawyer in private practice. She has successfully led complex global projects in democratic governance and public policy for institutional and multilateral clients, including the United Nations and the European Commission, and has worked in China, Ethiopia, Nepal, Rwanda, Sri Lanka, Sudan, Tajikistan, and Timor Leste. Pearl is Adjunct Professor at McGill's Faculty of Law and a Full Member of the McGill Centre for Human Rights and Legal. She serves as co-chair for the Canadian Centre for International Justice and is President of the Quebec Bar Association's Human Rights Committee. Pearl has published extensively on human rights and governance issues. Her monograph, *Speaking Out on Human Rights: Debating Canada's Human Rights System* won the 2015 Huguenot Society of Canada Award for freedom of expression and conscience. She is a senior fellow of the Raoul Wallenberg Centre for Human Rights and was named a Human Rights Changemaker by Equitas in 2017.

Rhoda E. Howard-Hassmann

Rhoda E. Howard-Hassmann is Professor Emeritus at Wilfrid Laurier University, where from 2003 to 2016 she held a Canada Research Chair in International Human Rights. She is a Fellow of the Royal Society of Canada, which in 2013 awarded her the John William Dawson Medal for Interdisciplinary Research. In 2006 she was named the first Distinguished Scholar of Human Rights by the Human Rights Section, American Political Science Association, and in 2014 she was named a Distinguished Scholar of Human Rights by the Human Rights Section of the International Studies Association. She is author of *Colonialism and Underdevelopment in Ghana* (1978), *Human Rights in Commonwealth Africa* (1986), *Human Rights and the Search for Community* (1995), *Compassionate Canadians: Civic Leaders Discuss Human Rights* (2003), *Reparations to Africa* (2008), *Can Globalization Promote Human Rights?* (2010), *State Food Crimes* (2016), and *In Defense of Universal Human Rights (2018)*. She is also co-editor of *International Handbook of Human Rights* (1987), *Economic Rights in Canada and the United States* (2006), *The Age of Apology: Facing Up to the Past* (2008), and *The Human Right to Citizenship: A Slippery Concept* (2015). She has been a visiting professor in South Africa, the Netherlands, the United States, and Sweden.

Gert Verschraegen

Gert Verschraegen is an Associate Professor in the Department of Sociology at the University of Antwerp. He has been a lecturer at the University of Leuven and a Visiting Scholar at Harvard University. His research interests centre on theoretical sociology, sociology of human rights, sociology of science and knowledge, and processes of transnationalization and Europeanization. Verschraegen is the co-editor of *Imagined Futures in Science, Technology and Society* (2017), *Making Human Rights Intelligible: Towards a Sociology of Human Rights* (2013), *Between Cosmopolitan Ideals and State Sovereignty: Studies in Global Justice* (2006), and *Divercities: Dealing with Diversity in Deprived and Mixed Neighbourhoods* (2018). He is a co-author of the book *Enabling Social Europe* (2006) and author of numerous articles on the sociology of human rights, sociological theory, and processes of transnationalization.

Index

ableism, and disability, 83

Aboriginal peoples: advocacy by, 23; clean water, 42, 68nn132–133; collective rights, 89; food insecurity, 129, 131; non-development of ancestral lands, 42; rights claims, 41–42, 44, 104; traditional medicine, 39, 67n120; underfunding on reserves, 46; violations of rights, 39; violence against women, 42, 68n135

abortion, as issue of rights, 23, 30

abstract humanity, recognition of, 13, 141–43

accessibility: and disabilities, 33–34; Internet accessibility, 38, 65n89, 103–4

accommodation: balance between public good and rights violations, 91–92. *See also* religion, and religious accommodation

accountability, in governance, 82, 85–86

age discrimination, 35, 37, 66n94

agency, and human rights, 7

"age of rights," 4

Ajzestat, Janet, 20

Alberta: censorship of press, 24

Alberta Human Rights Commission: pregnancy discrimination, 34

Allan, James, 4

Almrei, Hassan, 29

Alston, Philip, 5, 7, 15n17, 71n167

Amiel, Barbara, 27

Amnesty International, 47, 72n170

anti-Islamism, 26, 27, 60n37

anti-Semitism, 27, 60n36

Anti-Terrorism Act, 28, 29, 60n41, 61n47

arbitrary arrest and detention, 7, 16–17n30

Arbitration Act (Ontario), 25

assembly, freedom of: and accountability, 79; as colonial right, 19; as core right, 2, 7, 16–17n30, 125

Assembly of First Nations (AFN): Indigenous rights, 41–42, 68nn132–133, 68n135

assisted suicide, 31, 32, 65n89, 101, 105–6

association, freedom of: as colonial right, 19; as core right, 2, 7, 125; labour relations, 31, 63n65; and right to protest, 27, 59n34

Attawapiskat, rights claims, 41

Augustynowicz, Zbigniew, 35

autonomy, in assertion of rights, 4, 7, 8

Bagaric, Mirko, 4

Baker, David, 104

Barry, Brian, 45

basic rights. *See* core rights

BC College of Teachers, 25, 58n24

BC Human Rights Coalition: pregnancy discrimination, 34

BC Human Rights Tribunal: "hand-washing claim" (*Datt* case), 107–8; right to special education, 45–46, 71n163; textual harassment, 35
BC Métis Federation, 41
BC Poverty Reduction Coalition, 42
BC-Yukon Association of Drug Warrior Survivors, 37
Beaumont, Francine, 36
Beitz, Charles, 11, 69–70n150, 70n152
"Big Mike," 36
blogs, human rights, 40–41
B'nai Brith, 43
Boissoin, Stephen, 27
Borovoy, Alan, 99
British Columbia: *Human Rights Act*, 33, 64n74
British Columbia Civil Liberties Association: child pornography, distribution of, 1–2
British legal system: colonial definitions of rights, 19–20
Brodsky, Gwen, 85–86
bullying, 38, 39

Canada: anti-terrorism legislation, 28–29, 60–61nn41–42, 61nn44–45, 61n47; colonial definitions of rights, 19–20; Confederation, 20, 24; development of human rights legal system, 21–22; *French Services Act*, 81; historic overview of rights, 19–23; human rights protections, 115–16, 120n63; international obligations, 46–47; Lower Canada, 92 Resolutions, 19–20; postwar conception of, 21, 56n7; restrictions on religion, 19, 20; Safe Borders Agreement, 29, 61n45; wartime restrictions on civil liberties, 20–21. *See also legislation by name*
Canada Without Poverty, 38
Canadian Association for Community Living, 22

Canadian Association of the Deaf, 43
Canadian Charter of Rights and Freedoms: Aboriginal rights, 39, 67n120; consultation process, 23; and *Criminal Code*, 1–2, 31–32, 106; freedom of association, 31, 63n65; free speech, 9, 14n1; human rights as social construction, 128–29; international treaties, and Canadian law, 46, 71n165; law, and rights discourse, 1–2; legal rights, and due process, 14n2; limitations, 84, 94n16; linguistic rights, 80–81, 93n5; "notwithstanding clause," 92; refugee claimants (*Singh* case), 108–9, 118nn37–38; reinterpretation of rights, 31–33; relationship between legislative and judicial powers, 91–92, 95n24
Canadian Conference of Catholic Bishops, 43
Canadian Council of Muslim Women, 43
Canadian Human Rights Act, 104; hate speech, 27, 60n37; underfunding on reserves, 46
Canadian Human Rights Commission: underfunding on reserves, 46
Canadian Human Rights Tribunal: family status, 109–10
Canadian Labour Congress, 43
Canadian Museum for Human Rights: consultation process, 39–40; public hearings, 10
Canadian National Railway: employment standards law, 109–10
capitalism, rights as response to, 8
Carag, Eleanora, 42
censorship, 22; and criticism of government, 24; wartime use of, 20
charity, as moral value, 5
Charter of Quebec Values, 59n32
Charter of Secularism (France), 26, 58–59n28

child care: availability, 37, 43, 44; employer accommodation, 37

child pornography, distribution of, 1–2

children, 22; advocacy for, 23; child's best interests, 114; *Convention on the Rights of the Child* (1990), 103, 114; learning support, 39–40; of migrant workers, 103; right to nationality, 103

China: right to development, 62n58

Chinese Consolidated Benevolent Association, 19

Chong, Daniel, 15n8

Christian values, and racism, 19

Citizens for Safe Technology, 37

citizenship, as precondition for rights, 2, 20, 23

civic debate, undermining of by rights violations, 121

civil liberties: historical use of as term, 20, 56n5; *International Covenant on Civil and Political Rights* (1966), 103; and political rights, 19–20, 23; vs. social justice, 101–2; World Wars era, 20–21

civil rights, 13; and politics of absolutism, 134–35; state protection of, 140–41; vs. socio-economic rights, 138–41

clean water: access to, 31; as rights issue, 39, 42, 43, 68nn132–133

Clément, Dominique: CBC debate with Eliadis, 116n1

Cohen, Maxwell, 5

Cold War: politicized division of rights, 139, 144n11; security screening, 24–25

collective imaginaries, and rights claims, 141–43

collective rights, 89

compensation paid for rights violations, 84–85

compromise solutions: of competing rights claims, 136–37; and public policy, 5, 49, 80, 139; and

resource constraints, 123–24, 131; and rights analysis, 83, 86, 136–37

Confederation: religious accommodation, 20, 24

conscience, liberty of, 16–17n30

conservatives: alternative doctrine of human rights, 32; power of a phrase, appropriation of, 32, 63–64n71

Constitution Act, 1982, 80, 93n5

constitutional rights, international, 31

Convention on Economic, Social and Cultural Rights, 46–47

Convention on the Elimination of All Forms of Discrimination against Women, 103

Convention on the Rights of the Child (1990), 103, 114

Co-operative Commonwealth Federation (CCF): bill of rights campaign, 19, 57n8

core rights, 79, 124–25; as basic rights, 6, 16n23, 16n26; constitutional recognition of, 7; definitions of, 6–7; erosion of, 133–34; and fringe rights, 80; grievances as rights violations, 8, 17n35; historical contestation of, 125; in international human rights law, 114–15; political freedoms as, 2–3, 14n2; priority variation within, 138, 144n8; as problematic, 138–41; reinterpretation of rights, 137; and social justice issues, 11–12

Council of Canadians with Disabilities, 43; *VIA Rail* case, 112

Cranston, Maurice, 5, 15n6

Criminal Code: child pornography, 1–2; legal reform of, 1–2; overturning of criminal laws, 31–32, 106

Croatia, constitutional rights, 31

cultural retention as issue of rights, 23, 135

cultural traditions, and historical precedents of rights, 8–9

cyberbullying, 1, 14n1
Cyber-Safety Act (Nova Scotia), 1, 14n1

Datt, Beena, 107–8
David, Françoise, 44
day care: as issue of rights, 23; parental leave, 30, 62n53
Declaration of the Rights of Indigenous Peoples (UN), 41–42
democracy, rights as response to, 8
Desmond, Viola, 106
Des Rosiers, Nathalie, 12, 79–95, 124; concerns over silenced injustices, 79–80; deflationary pressures, 86–87; distinction between social justice and human rights, 82; inflationary rhetoric, 83–86; linguistic rights, 80–81, 93n5; rights analysis, aspects of, 83; rights as instruments of democratization, 88–92
Dickson, Brian, 71n165
disability, 22, 101; discrimination against, 36, 37; learning support for children with disability, 39–40, 112–14; Moore case implications, 83–86; *VIA Rail* case, 112
disability rights associations: accessibility issues, 33–34; advocacy by, 22, 23; social model vs. medical model, 51–52, 74n184
discrimination: on addiction, 36–37; age discrimination, 35, 37, 66n94; approaches to, as problematic, 38, 67n110, 79–80; disability, 36, 37; employment-based, 33, 37–38; family status, 37; gender bias, 35–36, 66n95; hate speech, 27; by landlords, 33, 34, 64n74; against non-citizens, 108–9, 118nn37–38; pregnancy discrimination, 34; prohibition of, 21–22; protected grounds, extension of, 104–5; race/national/ethnic origins, 46; and religious freedom, 24–26; as rights violation, 9, 22; sexual harassment, 32, 34–35, 36, 101,

105; sexual orientation, 33, 34, 36, 64n74, 101; social status, 36, 66n101; temporary foreign workers, 33; tree planters, 33
dissent, right to, 137
Donnelly, Jack, 16n26, 18n50, 126
Doukhobors, 24, 57–58n18
Douzinas, Costas, 51, 55, 73–74n179, 74n180
due process, 22; *Anti-Terrorism Act*, 28, 29, 60n41, 61n47; anti-terrorism legislation, 28–29, 60–61n42, 61n44, 61n47; as colonial right, 19; as core right, 2–3, 14n2, 125; and discriminatory policing, 79; *Emergencies Act*, 29; restrictions on, 20, 24, 28, 29; *War Measures Act*, 29
duty to accommodate, 84

Earle, Guy, 36
economic rights, 13, 16n23, 131; constitutional recognition of, 53, 75–76n193; permissible inequality, 123–24; and poverty, 79; as response to societal problems, 135; right of ownership, 135
education: denominational education, 24; as empowerment right, 127, 139; equality in, 83–86, 101; evolution of as right, 9; as issue of rights, 23; learning support for children with disability, 39–40, 83–86, 112–14; right to special education, 45–46, 71n163; safe schools, 41, 68n128; state responsibility to educate children, 113
Egale Canada: safe schools, 41, 68n128
Eliadis, Pearl, 97–120; allocation of resources, 111, 113, 123; CBC debate with Clément, 116n1; new rights claims, 12; right to education, 129; special education, 71n163
Elizabeth Fry Society, 43
Emergencies Act, 29

employment-based discrimination, 33, 37–38

employment standards law: caregiving, and family status, 109–10

empowerment: of new rights claims, 89–90, 93

empowerment rights, 127

end-of-life care, 101

enforced disappearances, prohibition of, 114

enforcement of global violations, 99

environment, and environmental concerns: constitutional protections, 48, 72–73n173; as issue of rights, 3, 38; as social justice issue, 10

equality, and equal treatment, 101, 110–14; as colonial right, 19–20; as core right, 2, 125; demands for, 9; gender bias, 35–36, 66n95; gender equality, 30, 34, 62n53, 64n79; permissible inequality, 123–24; question of meaning, 121; and sexual orientation, 105; and social justice, 44; and the socially disadvantaged, 55

expression, freedom of, 7

Facebook, 35; as vehicle for rights claims, 38, 41

fairness, as moral value, 5

family reunification, 23

family status, 109–10

feminist advocacy, 52, 75n188

Fenian Raids, 24

First Nations. See Aboriginal peoples

First Nations Child and Family Caring Society of Canada, 46

food, right to. See subsistence

food insecurity. See subsistence

foreign policy, and human rights, 22, 32

Forst, Rainer, 136–37

Frarer, Tom, 63–64n71

Freedman, Rose, 6, 16n24, 54–55

freedom of expression: and Internet accessibility, 103–4

freedom of information, 30–31, 63n62; International Right to Know Day, 30

freedom of movement, 7

freedom of speech, 110, 119n43; and accountability, 79; as colonial right, 19; as contested right, 9, 17n42, 24; as core right, 2, 16–17n30, 125; scope of, 27–28, 59n34; vs. hate speech, 27–28, 32

freedom of the person, 16–17n30

French Revolution, 17n41

French Services Act, 81

Friedman, Lawrence M., 17n42

Fudge, Judy, 74n186, 75n190

gay rights: in *Charter* consultation process, 22; conflict with religious beliefs, 26; and right to equality, 105; same-sex marriage, 26

Gaze, Beth, 76–77n201

Gearty, Connor, 6

gender-based violence, 39, 42, 43, 68n135; sexual assault laws, 53, 75n190; sexual inequality, 53, 75n191; systemic oppression of patriarchal societies, 52–53, 75n188

gender equality, 30, 34, 62n53, 64n79; *Convention on the Elimination of All Forms of Discrimination against Women*, 103

gender identity, 40, 41, 68n128–129

Gewirth, Alan, 74n180

Gill, Elizabeth A., 6, 16n23

Glasbeek, Harry, 74n186

Glendon, Mary Ann, 5–6

Globe and Mail: use of term "civil liberties," 20, 56n5; use of term "human rights," 3, 22

Gosepath, Stefan, 136–37

governance: alignment of public policy with legal obligations, 90–92, 94n22

government participation: as core right, 7

Great Blue Heron Charity Casino: gender bias, 35–36, 66n95

Greenpeace, 43

grievances: in *Charter* consultation process, 23; institutional framework for pursuance, 47–48; and language of rights, 37–38, 56, 76–77nn201–202, 133–34, 141–43; as new rights claims, 38–44; as rights violations, 2, 3, 8, 9–10, 14n4, 17n35; social movements involvement, 47–48

Griffin, James, 6, 13, 44, 47, 76–77nn201–202

Griffith, James, 7

Grodsky, Brian, 7

Gutmann, Amy, 6, 7, 13, 76–77n201

habeas corpus, 19; October Crisis, 24, 125; as protection right, 127; wartime suspension of, 20

Harper, Stephen, 119n43

Harris, Mike, 81

Hart, H.L.A., 4, 73–74n179

hate speech, 22; media opposition to legislation, 28, 60n39; prohibition of, 5; vs. free speech, 27–28, 32, 59n34

Hayward, Robert J., 63n62

health care: as issue of rights, 3, 23; l'Hôpital Montfort restructuring, 81, 94n8; and social justice, 44; state redistribution of resources, 53–54

Henkin, Louis: "age of rights," 4

hierarchy of rights: avoidance of, 51; civil liberties vs. social justice, 101–2; and patriarchal model of rights, 87; rejection of, 110, 115

Hitchens, Christopher, 58–59n28

Hodgson, Dorothy, 52–53, 75n191

Hodgson, Nancy, 70n152

Hoffman, Florian, 4–5

Hoffman, Stefan-Ludwig, 49–50

homelessness, and housing rights, 111–12

homosexuality. *See* gay rights; sexual orientation

housing, 22, 38, 41, 67n114, 110–12

Howard-Hassmann, Rhoda E., 121–32; core rights, 124–25, 128–29; human rights as social facts, 130; social democracy, 12–13; social justice, definitions of as problematic, 121–23

human flourishing, and human rights, 102, 117n16

human rights: as bottom-up phenomenon, 129; categories of rights, 126–27; definitions of, 3–4, 6–7; distinction from legal rights, 51, 73–74nn179–180; distinction from social justice, 10–12, 18n46, 54–56, 76–77nn201–202, 98–99; historical contingency of, 9, 17n40, 17n42, 134–37; and human flourishing, 102, 117n16; as indivisible, 13, 17n35, 138–41, 144n11, 144n15; as instruments of democratization, 88–92; interdependence of, 110, 124, 141; interpretations of, 36–37; laws vs. rights talk, 11, 18n48, 18n50, 49–50, 73n175; as modern invention, 8–9, 49, 57n10; plurality of, 135–36; print media use of term, 3, 5; role in facilitating social justice, 45–46; as social construction, 128–29; sociology of, 9–10; as universal principle, 23; war crimes, 5, 15n4

human rights commissions: critiques of, 106; legal challenges to, 90–91; media assault against, 107

human rights laws: dubious claims, fallacies of, 106–10; evolution of as response to new problems, 116; family status, 109–10; increased relevance of, 98; investments in programs and institutions generated, 100–101; political aspect of, 99–100; as reflection of public opinion, 129; successful new rights claims, 101

human rights violations: grievances, 2, 3, 8, 14n4, 17n35; in print media, 3, 20, 22, 56n5

Human Rights Watch, 6, 47, 50, 72n170

Hunt, Lynn, 9, 14, 17n40

Hutterites, 24, 57–58n18

Ignatieff, Michael, 6–7, 13, 16n26, 87

immigration, 22

Immigration Act: security certificates, 28–29, 61n44

immigration law: refugee claimants (*Singh* case), 108–9, 118nn37–38; refugee determination, 101

indivisibility of human rights, 13, 17n35

industrial democracy, 19

industrialization: and worker's rights, 8–9, 15n16

injustice: distinction from human rights, 2, 45; lived injustices of marginalized population, 79–80, 88–89

innocence, presumption of, 7

institutional infrastructure: in support of rights, 10

InStore, 37

International Bill of Human Rights: categories of rights, 126–27

International Covenant on Civil and Political Rights, 82, 103, 126, 138

International Covenant on Economic, Social and Cultural Rights, 116, 121–23, 139; housing rights, 110

international human rights law, 114–16; abstract values of, 46–47, 71n165; in Canada, 115–16, 120n63; categories of rights, 126–27; child's best interests, 114; core rights, 114–15; enforced disappearances, prohibition of, 114; hierarchy of rights, rejection of, 115; housing rights, 110–12; new rights claims, 5, 15n6; rights agreements, 15n9, 22; as top-down legal regime, 129; as unenforceable, 123

International Right to Know Day, 30

international treaties: abstract values of, 46–47, 71n165; growth in rights recognized, 30–31, 46–48

Internet: accessibility, 38, 65n89, 103–4; cyberbullying, 1–2

Islamic Institute of Civil Justice, 25

Jehovah's Witnesses, 24, 57–58n18

John Humphrey Centre for Peace and Human Rights, 41

Jones, Melinda, 76–77n201

Keegstra, James, 27, 60n36

Kindos, Ted, 36

Knipe, Patricia, 107

labour relations: blogs on, 41

labour rights, 31, 63n65; back-to-work legislation, 38

Lamarche, Gara, 87

Landman, Todd, 128–31

language of rights. *See* rights talk

law, and rights discourse, 1–2, 3, 11, 18n48, 18n50

left activism: association with human rights, 32, 63n68

Legal Education Action Fund, 53

legal equality, 121

legal studies: institutionalization of human rights, 10

legal systems: enforcement of global violations, 99; "frozen concepts" of law, 100

legislation: and rights inflation, 4, 15n9

lesbians and gays. *See* gay rights; sexual orientation

Levant, Ezra, *Shakedown*, 107

l'Hôpital Montfort restructuring: linguistic rights, 81, 94n8

liberal democracy: evolution of, 125; evolution of public consensus, 127–28; "thin"/"thick"

democracies, 128; vs. social democracy, 12–13, 126, 128–31
liberal rights: and social justice, 45
linguistic rights, 22, 23, 89; l'Hôpital Montfort restructuring, 81, 94n8; range of interpretation, 80–81, 93n5
live-in caregivers, 42
London School of Economics: Centre for the Study of Human Rights, 6
Luhmann, Niklas, 135

Mackenzie, William Lyon, 20
Maclean's magazine, 27, 107
MacNaughton, Heather, 113
Madsen, Mikael, 8, 10
Magna Carta, 19
Manitoba: pregnancy discrimination, 34
marginalized population: lived injustices as violation of rights, 79–80, 88–89
material equality, 121
material security, 126
McDonald's: "handwashing claim" against, 107–8
McGill Human Rights Interns' blog, 41
Mchangama, Jacob, 6, 16n24, 54–55
McIntosh, Lisa, 34–35
medical marijuana, 36
membership rights: communitarian principle of, 126–27
Menke, Christoph, 136–37
men's rights movement, 53
military intervention, 32
minimum wage, 23
minority rights: advocacy for, 23; denominational education, 24; religious freedom, 26
mobility: as issue of rights, 23
Molyneux, Maxine, 74n186
Moon, Richard, 27
Moore, Jeffrey: duty to accommodate, 84; equality in education, 83–86; right to special education, 39–40, 45–46, 71n163, 112–14

moral claims: as rights, 4
moral values: charity, 5; fairness, 5; and rights inflation, 47, 72n168; and social justice, 44, 45
Moyn, Samuel, 22, 23, 57n10

National Association of Women and the Law, 43; and men's rights movement, 53
nationality, right to, 102–3
Native Aboriginal Women's Association: violence against women, 42, 68n135
natural resources, 31
Neier, Aryeh, 6, 7, 50, 99
Nelson, Robert: Declaration of Independence, 20
Netflix, 38
new rights claims, 38–44; Aboriginal rights, 41–42, 68nn132–133, 68n135; adaptability of, 100; assisted suicide, 31, 32, 65n89, 101, 105–6; communication, 43, 103–4; as contributing to democratic debate, 125; costs of economic redistribution, 50–51; deflationary pressures, 86–87; dubious claims, fallacies of, 106–10; as empowering, 89–90; equality, and sexual orientation, 105; human rights blogs, 40–41; inflationary rhetoric, 83–86; Internet accessibility, 38, 65n89, 103–4; limited influence of, 142–43; as modern invention, 49; as natural democratic movement, 92–93; prisoners' rights, 43; protected grounds, extension of, 104–5; recognition of, 47, 71nn167–168; reinterpretation of rights, 136–37; rights evolution, 12, 102–6; and rights inflation, 4, 15n8; right to die, 65n89; right to nationality, 103; social movements, 41–44; as social process, 32–33; through social media, 40
newspapers. *See* print media

Norman, Ken, 115

Nova Scotia: *Cyber-Safety Act*, 1, 14n1; disabled accessibility issues, 33–34

Nova Scotia's Human Rights Commission: poverty as social condition, 40

Nowak, Manfred, 140–41

October Crisis: suspension of habeas corpus, 24, 125

Olorenshaw, Denis, 35

Ontario: *Arbitration Act*, 25; Human Rights Tribunal, 34; technology, role in sex discrimination, 35

Ontario Coalition Against Poverty (OCAP), 42

Ontario Human Rights Commission: disability, discrimination against, 36; employment-based discrimination, 37–38; Facebook, 38; mental disability, discrimination against, 34; technology, role in sex discrimination, 35, 65n89

Open Society, 6

Oxfam, 47

Parliament: Special Joint Committee on the Constitution, 23

Parsons, Rehtaeh, 1

Patriotes, Declaration of Independence, 20

permissible inequality, 123–24

physician-assisted death, 105–6. *See also* assisted suicide

PIVOT, 43

Pivot Legal Society, 38

plurality of human rights, 135–36

police powers, 22; preventative detention, 28, 60n41; racial profiling, 34; and right to protest, 59n34

political dissent: and banning of Internet access, 104

political equality, 121

political freedoms, 23; as core rights, 2–3; state protection of, 140–41

political human rights, 13

polygamy (Bountiful), 25

Posner, Eric, 5, 6, 13, 99

poverty: concerns over silenced injustices, 79–80; feminization of, 34, 64n81; and food insecurity, 129, 130, 131; as issue of rights, 3, 23, 24, 38, 39; poor with disabilities, 42; as social condition, 40, 131; as social justice issue, 10, 45

press, freedom of: as colonial right, 19; as core right, 2, 125; and criticism of government, 24; wartime censorship, 20

print media: opposition to hate speech legislation, 28, 60n39; use of term "civil liberties," 20, 56n5; use of term "human rights," 3, 5, 21–22, 57n8

prisoners: accommodation, 36, 66n100; advocacy for, 23, 40, 43

privacy, right to, 7, 22, 41, 136

property rights, 7, 57n8

prostitution: as violation of human rights, 43

protected grounds, extension of, 104–5

protection rights, 126–27

public good: and undifferentiated welfarism, 6

public hearings: Canadian Museum for Human Rights, 10

public policy: alignment of with legal obligations, 90–92, 94n22; and the good life, 121–22; litigation as influence on, 51, 74n181; and political compromise, 5, 49, 80, 83, 86, 139; "rationality" analysis, 91

quality of life, 41

Quebec: freedom of religion, 59n32; Hérouxville code of conduct, 59n32; racial profiling, 34; temporary foreign workers, 33

Quebec Human Rights Commission: accommodation, 36, 66n100; niqab/hijab complaints, 35

racial profiling, 34
racism: and Christian values, 19
rape shield law, 53, 95n24
Rawls, John, 14n4, 16–17n30
refugee determination, 101; *Singh* case, 108–9, 118nn37–38
reinterpretation of rights, 31–33
religion, and religious accommodation: anti-Islamism, 26, 27, 60n37; anti-Semitism, 27, 60n36; Charter of Quebec Values, 26, 59n32; Charter of Secularism (France), 26, 58–59n28; colonial restrictions on, 19, 20; in Confederation, 20, 24; discrimination against, 24, 57–58n18; hate speech, 27; historical precedents of rights, 8–9; as issue of rights, 23; opinions toward other religions, 30, 62n56; post-9/11, 30, 62n56; Trinity Western University, 25, 58n4, 58n25
religious freedom: *Arbitration Act* (Ontario), 25; as core right, 2, 7, 24–26, 125; and equality rights, 25, 26, 101; and the French Revolution, 17n41; Lord's Prayer conflict, 25; polygamy (Bountiful), 25; *sharia* law, 25
research, freedom of, 135
resources: impact of rights tribunals on, 84–85; state allocation of, 53–54, 111, 121, 131
rest and leisure: as issue of rights, 23
rights-based activism of social movements, 51–53, 74–75n186
rights inflation: additional implications, 54–55; constitutional protections, 48–49; and grievances, 2; inflationary rhetoric, 83–86; limited influence of, 142–43; and morality, 47, 72n168; negative connotation of, 92; prioritizing of claims, 50–51; reinterpretation of rights, 31–33; scholarly concerns, 4–7; as social process, 32–33. *See also* new rights claims

rights talk: abstract humanity, recognition of, 13, 141–43; evolution of, 5–6; in framing grievances, 37–38, 56, 76–77n201, 77n202, 133–34, 141–43; historical context of, 29–30; historic overview, 19–23; impact of popularization on, 3; and institutional accountability, 92; and new rights claims, 23; power of a phrase, appropriation of, 32, 63–64n71; and power of justice, 44; shift in terminology, 21–22, 57n8; and systemic social problems, 54; as transformative, 82; transformative power of, 90; and voice of minorities, 83–86; vs. "charitable"/religious talk, 89; vs. human rights law, 11, 18n48, 18n50, 49–50, 73n175; World Wars era, 20–21
right to development, 31
right to die, 65n89
right to life, 7, 32, 127
right to protest, 27, 59n34

Sachs, Albie, 110
Safe Borders Agreement, 29, 61n45
same-sex marriage, 26, 30; and freedom of religion, 33
Saskatchewan: Bill of Rights (1947), 21; labour relations, 31, 63n65; pregnancy discrimination, 34
Saskatchewan Federation of Labour: back-to-work legislation, 38
Save the Children, 47
scholarship: grievances as rights violations, 3, 14n4; rights-based activism, 51–53, 74–75n186, 75n188; rights inflation concerns, 4–7; rights talk, and institutional accountability, 92
Scott, F.R., 93
Secular Ontario: Lord's Prayer conflict, 25
security, as human right: as justification for repressive policies, 30, 62n58

security certificates, 28–29, 61n44

security of the person, 7

security screening: Cold War, 24–25

self-determination: as issue of rights, 23

Sen, Amartya, 7, 16–17n30; on social justice, 44–45

sexting, 35

sexual harassment, 32, 34–35, 36, 101, 105

sexual orientation: discrimination against, 33, 36, 64n74, 101; and gender identity, 40; and hate speech, 27; and right to equality, 105; and safe schools, 41, 68n128

Shue, Henry, 7, 16n26

Simpson, Jeffrey, 118n38

Sjoberg, Gideon, 6, 16n23

social activism: and rights advocacy, 81

social change: law as reflection of, 131

social democracy: categorization of rights, 126–27; food insecurity, 130, 131; "thin"/"thick" democracies, 128; vs. liberal democracy, 12–13, 126, 128–31

socialism, 19

social justice: accessibility to basic services, 109; conflation with human rights, 44–46, 69–70nn150–152, 88–90; costs of economic redistribution, 50–51; definitions of, as problematic, 121–23; degrees of urgency, 11; distinction from human rights, 54–56, 76–77nn201–202, 98–99; and the good life, 121–22; legal recognition of moral claims, 51, 73–74n179, 74n180; and morality, 44, 45; and public policy, 121; as pursuit of equality, 44; Rawls' theory of, 16–17n30; recognition of injustice, 10–12, 18n46; relation to social problems, 10; Sen on, 44–45; and socio-economic rights, 86–87; vs. civil liberties, 101–2

social media: cyberbullying, 1, 14n1; Facebook, 35, 40; framing of grievances as rights violations, 40; preservation of privacy, 136; Twitter, 40

social movements: anti-poverty organizations, 42; in Charter consultation process, 23; framing of grievances as rights violations, 4; rights-based activism, 51–53, 74–75n186; and social change, 22; use of rights talk, 47–48, 142–43; as vehicle for rights claims, 41–44; women's rights, 42–44

social practice: of rights, 3–4, 18n50

social rights: constitutional recognition of, 53, 75–76n193

social services: evolution of public consensus, 127–28; funding of, 46

social values: recognition of injustice, 18n46

socio-economic rights: deflationary pressures, 86–87; recognition of as human rights, 90; vs. civil rights, 138–41

sociology of human rights, 3–4, 9–10

South Africa: constitutional rights, 31; Government of South Africa v. Grootboom et al, 110–11

Speaking Out on Human Rights (Eliadis), 98, 100–101

Stammers, Neil, 73n175

state: alignment of public policy with legal obligations, 90–92, 94n22; allocation of resources, 53–54, 111; costs of economic redistribution, 50–51, 53–54; criticism of, and free speech, 9, 17n42, 24, 125–26; impact of rights tribunals on resources, 84–85, 121; restraint from government interference, 140–41; rights as justification for repression, 30–31, 62n58

state repression: colonial campaigns against, 19–20

Status of Women Canada, 34, 64n79

Steyn, Mark, 27, 59n35

subsistence: as core right, 7, 16n26; and food insecurity, 129, 130, 131; and right to food, 47, 122, 124, 127, 128

Supreme Court of British Columbia: *Abbotsford (City) v. Shantz*, 112; *Moore v. British Columbia*, 39–40, 45–46, 71n63, 83–86, 112–14

Supreme Court of Canada: assisted suicide, 32; family status, 109–10; "frozen concepts" of law, 100; hierarchy of rights, 110; judicial activism of, 111; labour rights, 31, 63n65; physician-assisted death, 105–6; reinterpretation of rights, 31–33; religion, and religious accommodation, 26; solicitation laws, 31–32; *Tanudjaja, et al. v. Attorney General of Canada, et al*, 111–12; Trinity Western University, 25, 58nn24–25

Supreme Court of Nova Scotia: cyberbullying, 1, 14n1

survival rights, 126–27

technology, role in sex discrimination, 35, 65n89

temporary foreign workers, 33, 34

terrorism: anti-terrorism legislation, 28–29, 60–61nn41–42, 61n44; contested rights, 24; defined, 28; electronic surveillance, 28; preventative detention, 28, 29, 61n47

text messaging, 33; sexting, 35

"thin"/"thick" democracies, 128

thought, freedom of, 7

Toronto Police Services: employment-based discrimination, 37–38

Toronto Star: use of term "human rights," 3

torture, freedom from, 7

Trinity Western University: pledge of conduct, 25, 58nn24–25

Twitter: as vehicle for rights claims, 40, 41

Union of BC Indian Chiefs: non-development of ancestral lands, 42

United Church, 43

United Nations: *Declaration of the Rights of Indigenous Peoples*, 41–42; Promotion and Protection of the Right to Freedom of Opinion and Expression (2011), 104; recognition of new rights claims, 47, 71n167; right to food, 122; Special Procedure mandates, 6, 16n24; Special Rapporteurs, 54–55, 104; water and sanitation as rights issue, 39

United States: Bill of Rights, 49; Safe Borders Agreement, 29, 61n45

Universal Declaration of Human Rights (1948), 30, 103, 126, 138; conflicts over interpretation, 136, 137

utilitarianism, 4

Vancouver 2010 Olympics: security zones, 31

Vancouver Rape Relief (VRR), 43

Vanhala, Lisa, 51, 74n181, 74n184

Verschraegen, Gert, 8, 10, 124, 128, 133–44; abstract humanity, recognition of, 13, 141–43; core rights, 138–41; historical contingency of rights, 134–37; rights claims, rise of, 141–43

victims' bill of rights, 32

Vienna Declaration and Programme of Action, 144n11

violence against women, 39, 42, 43, 68n135

voting rights, 2

war crimes tribunals, 5, 15n4

War Measures Act, 29

war on terror. *See* terrorism

water. *See* clean water

welfare, 7

West Coast Legal Education and Action Fund, 42–43

Whatcott, Bill, 27

Williams, Norma, 6, 16n23

Wilson, Bertha, 118n37

Wilson, Richard, 18n48, 51

Winnipeg Free Press: use of term "civil liberties," 20, 56n5; use of term "human rights," 3, 22

women: advocacy by, 23, 52, 75n188

Women Against Violence Against Women, 43

women's rights, 43, 101; child care, 37, 43, 44; in colonial Canada, 20; *Convention on the Elimination of All Forms of Discrimination against Women*, 103; family status, 109–10; female prisoners, 43; feminization of poverty, 34, 64n81; and the French Revolution, 17n41; gender equality, 30, 34, 62n53, 64n79; pay equity, 44; pregnancy discrimination, 34; rape shield law, 53; violence against women, 39, 42, 43, 68n135; and workforce participation, 8–9

work, 22

workers' rights: back-to-work legislation, 38; emergence of, 8–9, 15n16, 21; labour law blogs, 41; right to strike, 31, 63n65; wartime restrictions, 20

workplace violations, 41

Yergeau, Robert, 94n8

Yukon Human Rights Commission: right to housing, 38, 67n114

YWCA, 43

Zundel, Ernst, 27